Apple Pro Training Series

GarageBand

Mary Plummer

Apple
Certified

Apple Pro Training Series: GarageBand
Mary Plummer
Copyright © 2015 by Peachpit Press

Peachpit Press
www.peachpit.com

To report errors, please send a note to errata@peachpit.com.
Peachpit Press is a division of Pearson Education.

Apple Series Editor: Lisa McClain
Project Editor: Nancy Peterson
Production Coordinator: Kim Elmore, Happenstance Type-O-Rama
Development Editor: Eric Schumacher-Rasmussen
Technical Editor: Klark Perez
Copy Editor: Liz Welch
Proofreader: Darren Meiss
Compositor: Cody Gates, Happenstance Type-O-Rama
Indexer: Jack Lewis
Cover Illustration: Mimi Heft
Cover Production: Cody Gates, Happenstance Type-O-Rama

ISBN 13: 978-0-133-90092-7
ISBN 10: 0-133-90092-4
9 8 7 6 5 4 3 2 1
Printed and bound in the United States of America

Contents at a Glance

Table of Contents

Getting Started

Welcome to the official training course for GarageBand, Apple's totally redesigned and more-powerful-than-ever music recording and arrangement software. This book is for everyone from the beginner just curious about music creation to the seasoned professional who happens to be new to GarageBand. Even if you have been using the previous versions of GarageBand for years, this book is packed with all-new projects and features that you'll want to learn.

Leave all apprehension behind. This isn't a manual that goes step-by-step through every button, instrument, and preference. Nor is it a cursory tour that detours at will through GarageBand with no particular direction in mind. Rather it is a guided, in-depth, hands-on workshop to immerse you in GarageBand and many of the application's exciting and powerful recording, arranging, music-making, fixing, mixing, and sharing tools.

You don't need a background in music or any musical instruments or equipment other than a Mac. However, if you happen to have some instruments around, you'll be invited to play and record them. And for those of you who have always dreamed of learning to play piano or guitar, Bonus Lesson 1, "Learning to Play Piano and Guitar with GarageBand," walks you through GarageBand's first learn-to-play lesson.

There is also a bonus GarageBand for iOS overview lesson that shows you how to create projects, change instruments, record, add loops, mix, save, and share your GarageBand for iOS projects via iCloud. You can find both bonus lessons online on the same page as the lesson files.

What GarageBand Does for You

Recording, arranging, and sharing original music were once daunting and costly endeavors that required a lot of money, time, and resources to accomplish.

GarageBand allows you to create music your way, at your own pace, giving you all of the tools you need to accomplish your finished song with no time pressure, budget restraints, or critics to hinder your progress. Best of all, GarageBand offers tools for fixing timing, pitch, and groove to improve your recorded performances.

With GarageBand and your Mac, you have a fully functioning recording studio and music workshop. How is it a workshop? Because you can also learn to play piano or guitar, design and build your own electric guitar amp and pedalboard with stompboxes, and create customized effects. Using GarageBand as a recording studio, you can attach a MIDI keyboard to play and record MIDI Software Instruments—or simply play your computer keyboard with Musical Typing. You can connect an electric guitar or bass directly through the Audio-in port or through a third-party audio interface depending on your Mac inputs and configuration. Or you can use the built-in mic on your Mac to record your instrument or vocals. Regardless of the input, once you record your tracks you can easily edit your recordings, add effects, and arrange and mix your music. If you like writing songs, you can just record your rough tracks and use the handy Note Pad to jot notes or lyrics. There's even a dictation feature so you can speak your lyrics and they will be typed for you.

You may already use your Mac for communication with friends and family through email and to collect and organize your photo and movie memories with iPhoto and iMovie. Chances are iTunes already holds and organizes all your favorite songs. Why not add a playlist of your own original music? With GarageBand on your Mac, you can fulfill your musical aspirations as well and share the finished songs to iTunes, iCloud, or even the world through SoundCloud.

This book isn't about learning software and memorizing shortcuts, menus, and buttons. It's about creating music, working with music, building music, and making all types of music sound great. As you explore different projects ranging from a little dog-walking ditty (recorded on an iPhone while walking a dog—really) to a recording session with a professional guitarist, to creating a loopy ringtone, you'll end up learning the shortcuts and software along the way.

The Methodology

This book emphasizes hands-on training. Each exercise is designed to help you learn the application inside and out, starting with the basic interface and moving on to advanced music editing, arranging, and mixing techniques. If you are new to GarageBand, it would be helpful for you to start at the beginning and progress through each lesson in order, since each lesson builds on information learned in previous ones. If you are already familiar with GarageBand, you can start with any section and focus on that topic. However, since GarageBand has been totally redesigned, even the seasoned GarageBand users will discover new features and insights in the earliest lessons.

The projects you'll work with were carefully designed as practical exercises. They aren't big-budget music recordings to show off the software. These are real-life examples, created with real people and no additional budget to demonstrate some of the range of projects you can do yourself with GarageBand.

GarageBand Course Structure

Each of the nine lessons in this book focuses on a different aspect of creating projects with GarageBand. Each lesson expands on the basic concepts of the program, giving you the tools to use GarageBand for your own projects.

The lessons in this book can be informally divided into seven sections:

▶ Lessons 1–2: Learning the interface and working in the timeline.

▶ Lesson 3: Working with pre-recorded Apple Loops and arranging music

▶ Lessons 4–7: Recording, editing, and adding effects to different types of instruments and tracks, including MIDI Software Instruments, vocal audio tracks, electric guitar, and drum and percussion tracks

▶ Lesson 8: Mixing and adding EQ effects to complete a project

▶ Lesson 9: Sharing your finished projects

▶ Bonus Lesson 1: Learning to Play Piano and Guitar with GarageBand

▶ Bonus Lesson 2: Working with GarageBand for iOS—an overview of recording, playing, and sharing music on your iOS device

System Requirements

This book was written using GarageBand 10 on OS X Mavericks. However, the project files and lessons are compatible with both Mavericks and Yosemite operating systems for the Mac. If you have an older version of GarageBand, you will need to upgrade to the current GarageBand version to follow along with every lesson. At the time of this printing, the GarageBand software is free with any new Macintosh computer and OS X Mavericks.

The free version of GarageBand includes one Drummer, 50 Software Instrument sounds, and 500 loops. There is an optional one-time GarageBand in-app purchase that includes an additional 17 drummers, 150 software instrument sounds, and 1,500 loops.

The step-through exercises in this book do not require the purchased upgrade. The system used to create the projects in this book was fully loaded with the in-app purchase so the screenshots may not always match your screen.

Occasionally, there will be a bonus exercise, or a sample of a finished version of a song where I took advantage of the additional sounds and loops. You will be advised in those cases that if you have the additional download installed, you can open up a sample project to see and hear my final version of the project. In some cases, such as the electric guitar recording session project in Lesson 6, there will be two versions of the project. One version will include the drummer track that the guitarist used for his actual recording. The other version will include the default drummer track that does not require the in-app purchase. Regardless, both versions of the project will follow the identical steps and include the identical regions.

Before you begin the lessons in this book, you should have a working knowledge of your Mac, OS X , your iPhone or iPad, and iOS 7. You don't need to be an expert, but you do need to know how to use the mouse and standard menus. Those of you with GarageBand for iOS who wish go through Bonus Lesson 2 should have a basic knowledge of how to use your iPhone or iPad and how to use an iOS 7 touch screen.

What do you need to know about your Mac before starting? It would be helpful if you are comfortable with opening, saving, and closing apps and files on the Mac, as well as how to tap, swipe, and click your mouse or trackpad. You will need a working understanding of how OS X organizes files on your computer. If you need to review any of these techniques, see the printed or online documentation that came with your device.

Copying the GarageBand Lesson Files

The *Apple Pro Training Series: GarageBand* lesson files must be downloaded to your Mac in order to complete the lessons in this book. After you save the files to your hard disk, each lesson will instruct you in their use.

To download these files, you must have your book's access code, which is provided on a card in the back of the printed editions of this book and on the "Where Are the Lesson Files?" page in electronic editions.

For complete download instructions, see "Downloading GarageBand Projects for This Book" in Lesson 1.

Resources

Apple Pro Training Series: GarageBand is not intended to be a comprehensive reference manual, nor does it replace the documentation that comes with the application. Rather, the book is designed to be used in conjunction with other comprehensive reference guides. These resources include:

▶ The companion Peachpit website: As GarageBand is updated, Peachpit may choose to update lessons as necessary. Please check www.peachpit.com/aptsgb.

▶ The Apple website: www.apple.com

▶ The Reference Guide: Accessed through the GarageBand Help menu, the Reference Guide contains a complete description of all features.

▶ *Apple Pro Training Series: iPhoto* (Peachpit, 2014), by Dion Scoppettuolo, is an excellent companion to this book. Learn how to use iPhoto to enhance your photos, create slideshows, and print keepsake photo books on both Mac OS X and iOS.

▶ *Apple Pro Training Series: iMovie* (Peachpit, 2014), also by Dion Scoppettuolo, is an excellent companion to this book. Learn how to use iMovie to create first-class movies, advanced slideshows, and fun movie trailers on both OS X and iOS.

Acknowledgments

We would like to thank the following individuals for their contributions of media used throughout the book:

Casey Brassard, for playing along with his guitar in the "Learning to Play Piano and Guitar with GarageBand" and "Working with GarageBand for iOS" bonus lessons.

Tina Sacco, for her award-winning poems "Life's Flower" and "Groundhog Day," as well as her spoken voice reading of her work.

Chad Waronicki, for his electric guitar riffs and expertise.

Lauren Diaz and Brooke Bingham, for letting us record and use their award-winning hip-hop dance, as well as choreographer William Blair and Tonya Matheny for her support and use of the Ready Set Dance studio.

Kathryn Perez, for her wah-vocal and kazoo recordings used in the recording electric guitar without a guitar section.

Klark Perez, for editing the Lexie walking and RSD The Step Off video clips used in this book.

Ben Estes, for his insights and suggestions as well as the Follow and Groove Track demo projects.

Colby Stiltz, for his hip-hop tempo tips and tricks.

The amazing Peachpit team: Eric Schumacher-Rasmussen, Liz Welch, Nancy Peterson, Darren Meiss, and Kim Wimpsett, for their input and efforts in crafting this book.

1

Lesson Files	APTS GarageBand Book Files > Lesson 01 > 1-1 Scales Starting, 1-2 Cycle and Horns, 1-3 Scales Tasks, 1-4 Scales Finished
Time	This lesson takes approximately 60 minutes to complete.
Goals	Explore the GarageBand window
	Navigate in the timeline
	Understand tracks and regions
	Explore the Library and change a patch
	Explore the Smart Controls pane and add reverb to a track
	Explore the editors
	Create a cycle area
	Show the loop browser
	Audition a loop and add it to the project
	Change a track name and icon

Working with a GarageBand Project

GarageBand has been completely reimagined, reengineered, and remixed into an (even more powerful and still user-friendly) personal music workshop and recording studio.

Whether you're an accomplished musician, a hobbyist, or simply someone who's always wanted to try your hand at making music, GarageBand can help you take your musical aspirations to the next level—no experience or additional equipment required!

In this lesson, you'll take a guided tour of the GarageBand basic interface and learn how to use the transport controls, navigate in the timeline, audition Apple Loops, add a loop region, and show and hide the browser, editors, and Library. Along the way you'll also learn some valuable tips for advanced navigation and managing your workspace.

Downloading GarageBand Projects for This Book

The downloadable content for *Apple Pro Training Series: GarageBand* includes the project files you will use for each lesson, as well as media files that contain additional audio, video, or text you will need for each exercise. After you save the files to your hard disk, each lesson will instruct you in their use.

This book is written as project-based, step-by-step instruction manual. It is designed using specific prebuilt GarageBand projects and media. Throughout the book you will be encouraged to try what you've learned on your own projects.

The Apple Pro Training Series: GarageBand lesson files download includes all the projects and media files you'll need to complete the lessons in this book.

To install the GarageBand lesson files:

1   Connect to the Internet, navigate to www.peachpit.com/redeem, and enter your access code.

 If you are working with a printed edition of the book, the access code is provided on the card at the back of the book.

 If you are working with an electronic version of the book, the access code number is on the "Where Are the Lesson Files?" page.

 NOTE ▸ If you purchase or redeem a code for the electronic version directly from Peachpit, the lesson file link will automatically appear on the Lesson & Update Files tab without the need to redeem an additional code.

2   Click Redeem Code, and sign in or create a Peachpit.com account.

3   Locate the downloadable files on your Account Page under the Lesson & Update Files tab.

4   Click the lessons file link and download the APTS GarageBand Lessons.zip to your Downloads folder.

 NOTE ▸ Once you enter the redeem code, you can download the APTS GarageBand Lessons.zip as many times as you like for your account.

5   After downloading the file, open your Downloads folder, and double click APTS GarageBand Lessons.zip to unzip it.

Following these steps will copy the APTS GarageBand Book Files folder to your desktop. This folder contains the lesson files used in this book; each lesson has its own folder.

Opening and Saving a GarageBand Project

For this lesson about the GarageBand Interface, you'll need to open the **1-1 Scales Starting** project and save it to a new folder where you will save all of your work throughout this book.

You can open GarageBand projects from your computer or within GarageBand. Since you just downloaded and installed the projects to your computer, let's open this first project from the lessons folder on your desktop.

1   Quit GarageBand, if it is still open from the previous lesson.

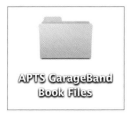

2   On your computer's desktop, locate the APTS GarageBand Book Files folder, and double-click the folder to open it in the Finder. There you will see a folder for each lesson, as well as the Additional Media and Lesson Bonus Projects folders.

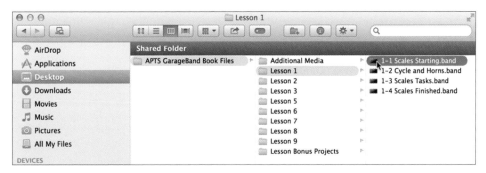

NOTE ▶ Your Finder view may differ from the view shown in the screenshot, but the contents of the APTS GarageBand Book Files folder should be the same.

3   Double-click the Lesson 1 folder to see all of the projects for this lesson. Double-click the project **1-1 Scales Starting** to open it in GarageBand.

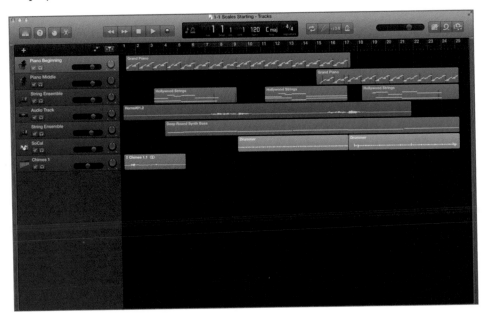

When GarageBand opens, you will see a large window containing all the elements for the **1-1 Scales Starting** project.

Before we play the song, or make any changes to the interface, let's save the project.

4   Choose File > Save As to open the Save As dialog.

NOTE ▸ To expand the Save As dialog, click the down arrow at the right side of the Save As field.

5 Click the Desktop icon in the sidebar (left side) of the Save As dialog to select the desktop as the location to save your project.

6 In the lower-left corner of the dialog, click the New Folder button. A New Folder dialog opens.

7 In the "Name of new folder" field, enter *My GarageBand Projects*. Click Create. The new folder appears on your desktop.

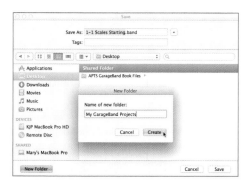 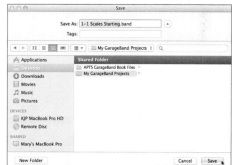

8 In the Save As dialog, click Save.

That's it. You saved a copy of the project that you can freely modify throughout the lesson, while retaining the original version in the lesson folder.

Exploring the GarageBand Window

Among the many advantages of GarageBand is the simplicity of its interface. GarageBand uses one window as the base of operations. This window is your recording studio and music workshop.

Hidden within this window are various multipurpose areas (panes) and tools that you will work with later. For now, it's a good idea to get familiar with the basic GarageBand window areas.

Control bar   LCD display

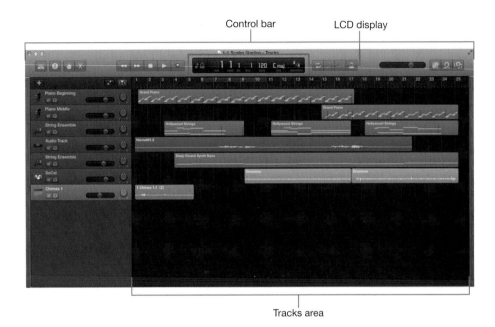

Tracks area

The basic areas of the GarageBand window are as follows:

▶   **Control bar**—The light gray area at the top of the GarageBand window that includes the transport controls for controlling playback of the project, an LCD (liquid crystal display) showing project properties and time format, buttons to show and hide the various areas of GarageBand, and buttons for frequently used tools and commands

▶   **LCD Display**—The black display in the center of the control bar showing project properties, time format, and playhead position

▶   **Tracks area**—The workspace where you record audio and MIDI regions, as well as add and arrange Apple Loops and other media files to build a project

Understanding the Tracks Area

The Tracks area is your primary workspace, so you will be learning it more in depth with each lesson. For now, it is important to understand the elements of the Tracks area so you will know how it works.

▶   **Tracks**—Horizontal lanes that are aligned to time positions on a ruler and grid. These lanes (tracks) contain individual musical parts, or regions, as performed by a particular instrument. All audio, MIDI, and drummer regions for a project are contained in tracks.

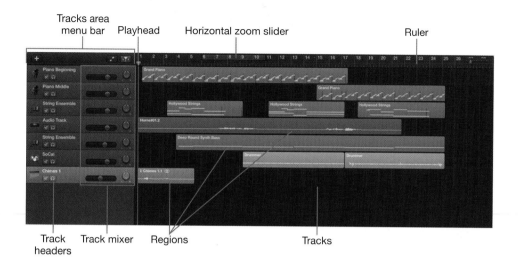

Tracks area menu bar · Playhead · Horizontal zoom slider · Ruler

Track headers · Track mixer · Regions · Tracks

▶ **Regions**—These are the building blocks of a project and contain individual musical parts (regions) from a particular instrument. An instrument track may contain only one region, or it may contain many smaller regions—individual takes and retakes, often called *overdubs*.

▶ **Track headers**—A header shows the instrument icon and name to the left of each instrument track. The track headers also include a Mute button to silence a track, a Solo button to silence all other tracks, and other functions that can be shown or hidden, such as arming the track for recording.

▶ **Track mixer**—This includes a volume slider for adjusting the track volume and a pan wheel to adjust the position of the track in the left-to-right stereo field.

▶ **Ruler**—This runs horizontally along the top of the tracks area/timeline. It shows musical time in bars (measures) and beats or standard time in minutes and seconds for nonmusical projects.

▶ **Timeline**—This is another name for your music recording and arranging workspace. The timeline consists of a horizontal track for each instrument. It graphically represents linear time from left to right using a beat ruler at the top of the window. The far-left edge of the timeline represents the beginning of a song.

▶ **Playhead**—This shows exactly what part of the song is currently playing. The playhead is a triangle (with a long vertical line underneath) on the beat ruler. During playback the playhead moves from left to right along the timeline, playing the regions that it touches. In addition to playing the regions, it can be used as a position indicator for the LCD display, as well as a tool to determine where to record, cut, copy, and paste music regions with the timeline.

▶ **Tracks area menu bar**—This is a dark gray bar running across the top of the tracks area that includes controls for adding tracks and showing track automation, as well as a Catch button and horizontal zoom slider.

▶ **Horizontal zoom slider**—This slider is handy for adjusting the horizontal zoom of the timeline workspace.

You'll work with each area in the next few lessons. For now, let's start with the transport controls in the control bar and play the project.

Navigating and Controlling Playback

There are several ways to play a project. In fact, many GarageBand features can be accessed by menu, button, or keyboard shortcut. The transport control buttons are located in the control bar next to the LCD display.

1   Press the Spacebar, or click the Play button in the control bar to play the song. Notice that the Play button turns green during playback.

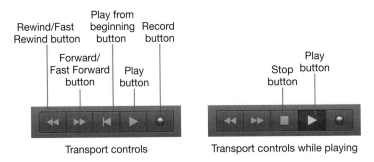

Transport controls   Transport controls while playing

As the music plays, you will see the playhead move from left to right along the timeline.

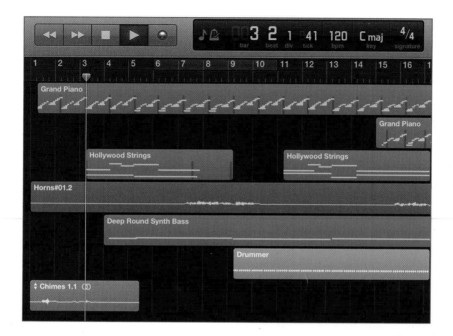

NOTE ▶ This project is part of a routine piano scales exercise that was partially orchestrated to demonstrate the simplicity of the orchestration process in GarageBand. Nearly every music student has at one time or another (perhaps daily) had to practice fingering by playing major scales (regardless of the instrument). Therefore, it seems fitting that your first project to learn the basic GarageBand interface involves scales as well. However, instead of using this project to hone your musical skills, you will use it to become more proficient in playing GarageBand projects and navigating the interface.

2   When the music is over, click the Stop button or press the Spacebar to stop playback.

3   Press Return to return the playhead to the beginning of the song.

That's all there is to playing a project straight through.

Positioning the Playhead in the Ruler

What if you want to start playback from a specific point in the timeline? No problem. You can simply drag the playhead to a new position or click the ruler to move it to that position. Just be sure to click the lower part of the ruler in the playhead area to move the playhead. Clicking the upper part of the ruler (marked with numbers) will turn on Cycle mode (which you will use when working with a cycle region later in the lesson). For now, stick to clicking the lower part of the ruler.

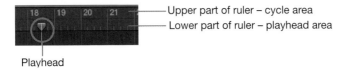

Upper part of ruler – cycle area
Lower part of ruler – playhead area

Playhead

1   Click anywhere on the lower part of the ruler to move the playhead to that position.

2   Drag the top of the playhead left and right in the playhead area of the ruler. As you drag, you can see the LCD display change based on the current playhead position.

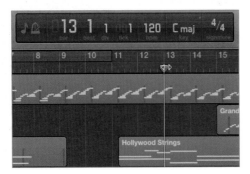

NOTE ▸ If you see a yellow cycle area in the upper part of the ruler, or the yellow Cycle button in the Control bar is turned on, click the Cycle button to turn it off before proceeding with the exercise.

3   Double-click the ruler just before the first Hollywood Strings region in the Hollywood Strings track to begin playback at that position.

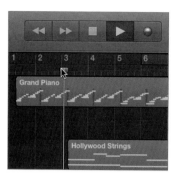

4   Stop playback. Press Return to move the playhead back to the beginning of the song.

Well done. In just a few clicks you've mastered the art of GarageBand playback.

Exploring the Workspace, Tracks, and Regions

Now that you've played the project, let's take a closer look at the different musical parts and tracks that make up the song.

The project **1-1 Scales Starting** includes seven tracks, each containing a different musical instrument part. The color of a region indicates the type of region and instrument recording. You can usually figure out at a glance which instrument parts are in each track based on the icon and instrument name in the track headers.

1   Look at the track headers for each track. Chances are they are all obvious except the track in the middle (the fourth track from the top) called Audio Track.

2   Click the empty space in the header of the track called Audio Track to select that track.

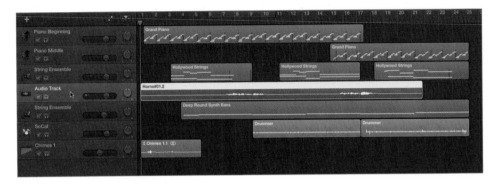

The selected track header brightens to indicate it has been selected. Also, all of the regions within that track (in this case one region) are automatically selected. You can easily identify a selected region because it brightens as well.

3   While the region is selected, look for the region's name in the illuminated bar at the top of the region.

As you can see the region is named Horns#01.2.

NOTE ▶ The #01.2 in the name Horns#01.2 is a GarageBand naming convention to indicate it is the second instance (.2) that the Horns#01 recording has been used in this project. From now on in this book I'll just use the region name without the information followed by a # sign or decimal pont—unless it is significant to the lesson.

Aha. It must be a horns track. Technically it is a recording of a horns part, though it was actually a sampled horn sound played by an external keyboard and recorded with a microphone into GarageBand as an audio track as though it were an acoustic instrument. What is an audio track? Read on; you'll find out in the next section.

4   Click anywhere in the empty workspace (the dark gray area) to deselect the region.

TIP ▶ It is a good idea to always deselect regions when they don't need to be selected. Otherwise, selected items can be accidentally cut, copied, pasted, moved, or deleted. Don't worry; you'll learn how to work with all of these features in time, including advanced selecting and editing.

Identifying Regions and Tracks

A track can include audio regions, MIDI regions called Software Instruments or Drummer regions, and can be easily identified by the color of the regions within the track.

Regions come in a variety of sizes and colors (according to type):

▶ **Audio regions**—Appear as purple, blue, yellow, or orange regions depending on how the audio files were recorded or added to the project. You can record live audio parts into GarageBand using the built-in microphone on your Mac, or a microphone, guitar, or keyboard that's plugged into the audio-in port on your Mac. You can also record audio parts through other input devices that you connect to your computer. Imported audio files appear as orange regions. Regardless of the color of the region, all audio track regions include a visual audio waveform to illustrate the recorded sound.

Recorded guitar or bass (purple)

Recorded instrument through microphone, or audio Apple Loop (blue)

Drummer track (yellow)

Imported audio file (orange)

▶ **MIDI regions (Software Instruments)**—Appear as green regions and are recorded using a USB music keyboard, a MIDI synthesizer–type keyboard, the GarageBand onscreen keyboard, or Musical Typing with the GarageBand software and your computer's keyboard as the MIDI instrument. All Software Instrument regions include visual MIDI note events to illustrate the recorded notes.

MIDI Software Instrument recording or Apple Loop (green)

Exploring the Library

So far you have only been working with the basic GarageBand window areas. In the next series of exercises you will look at the Library to become familiar with using it for identifying and changing the sound of a track. You will also learn to show or hide the Library as needed while you learn the GarageBand interface.

The Library button is located at the far-left of the toolbar and looks like a library bookshelf.

Let's start by showing the Library, and rather than use the button you will try the most intuitive method and double-click the region.

1   Double-click the empty space in the Piano Beginning header (Track 1). The Library appears in the left side of the GarageBand window.

The Library shows the Track icon (in this case a Steinway Grand Piano) that represents the current instrument (patch) assigned to the selected track.

2   Click the empty space in the Audio Track header to show that track in the Library. This time, there is no instrument picture because no patch (instrument sound preset) has been added to the original horn recording.

Search field   Track icon

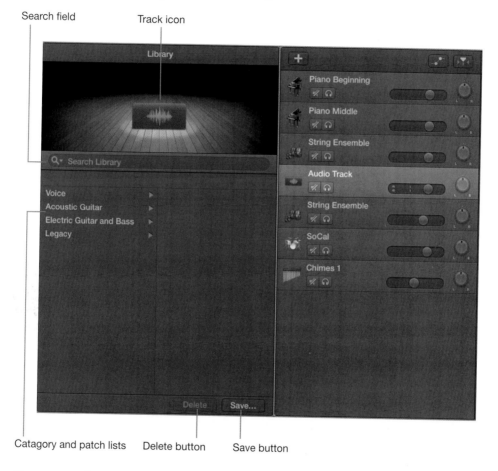

Catagory and patch lists   Delete button   Save button

You can use the Library to change a patch, save a patch, or search for different available patches and then change a patch. You will work with this in depth in other lessons. For now let's just change the patch to a Classic Vocal to enhance the sound. Why would you apply a vocal patch to a horn sound? Because the patches for audio tracks are limited to Voice, Acoustic Guitar, and Electric Guitar and Bass. Since vocal patches are based on types of microphones and basic effects commonly applied to vocals, they can also be applied to any acoustic instrument.

NOTE ▸ If you had a previous version of GarageBand installed on your computer before installing this version, you will see a Legacy category in your Instrument list that includes patches from previous versions.

3   Move the playhead in the timeline to the middle of the sixth measure (bar 6)—right before the waveform of the horn begins within the Horns region. Otherwise you'll have to wait for playback to reach that part of the song to hear the new patch.

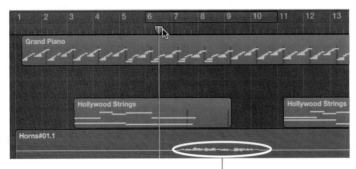

Audio waveform of horn recording

4   In the Library patch list, click the Voice category and the Classic Vocal patch. Instantly the track name and icon changes accordingly.

NOTE ▸ If you select the name field, or type a new track name, the track name will not change according to the selected patch.

5   Play the song starting at bar 6 to hear the Classic Vocal patch. If you were expecting the horn recording to sound like vocals, it doesn't. In fact, you may or may not hear the difference right away. The best way to do that is to compare the patches by playing one, then the other.

6   Click the Natural Vocal patch and play that section of the song again. Stop playback.

Of course, manually moving the playhead each time you want to play a section of a song over and over would be tedious and frustrating. Luckily, you can use something called a cycle area to accomplish the same feat without the repetitive clicking.

Using a Cycle Area

There are many uses for a cycle area in GarageBand. For this exercise you'll turn on Cycle mode and create a cycle area over the first horn waveform to make it easier to compare the various vocal patches while it plays.

1   Press C, or click the Cycle mode button to turn on the cycle area.

The cycle area is displayed as a yellow strip in the upper part of the ruler. You can drag the center of the cycle area to move it horizontally, or drag the edges to resize it.

2   Drag the edges of the current cycle area so that it starts at bar 7 and ends at bar 10 to create a cycle area over the first horn part in the song.

3   Start playback. Only the part of the song within the cycle area plays—over and over.

4   In the Library, click the Bright Vocal patch to hear it. Next try the Classic Vocal patch. Feel free to experiment with any of the Vocal patches in the Voice category to hear how they sound. No matter which patch you select, the track still sounds like a horn and not a vocal recording. That's because changing the patch of an audio track doesn't change the instrument; it only changes the effects applied to that track to enhance the sound.

NOTE ▶ To me, all of the Vocal patches sound good for this track (except Telephone Vocal and Fuzz Vocal). The Bright Vocal patch is very bright and present, whereas the Classic Vocal sounds warmer and somehow seems more balanced with the strings and piano. Keep in mind that everybody's musical taste is different.

5   Click the Classic Vocal patch if it is not already selected and stop playback.

So now you know how to show and use the Library patches as well as create and play a cycle area. What this track could really use is some reverb, to make the horns sound more distant and in a larger space instead of right behind you, blaring in your ear. To add reverb you'll need the Smart Controls pane.

Exploring the Smart Controls Pane

The bottom of the GarageBand window is reserved for the Smart Controls pane and the editors used to make precision changes to regions and their contents. In this exercise we'll take a quick look at the Smart Controls pane and use it to add reverb to the Horns audio region. You'll work more with the Smart Controls pane in later lessons.

To show the Smart Controls pane, you can click the Smart Controls button, press B, or choose View > Show Smart Controls. For this exercise you'll use the Smart Controls button. Keep in mind that Smart Controls are track-based, so make sure you have the right track selected before you make any changes to the controls.

1   Select the Classic Vocal track header, if it is not already selected. Remember, this is the audio track containing the horns region.

2   Click the Smart Controls button to show the Smart Controls pane at the bottom of the window.

▶   **Inspector button**—Displays the Smart Controls inspector.

▶   **Screen controls**—Let you modify the sound of the track. Not only do they look like physical controls on actual devices in a real music studio environment, they respond like them as well. Labels on each control make the functions easy to understand.

▶ **Smart Control inspector**—Shows monitoring and input controls for audio tracks, and a keyboard sensitivity control for Software Instrument tracks.

▶ **Master button**—Displays Smart Controls for the master track. Any changes applied to the master track modify the sound of the entire song.

▶ **Compare button**—Click this button to see a before-and-after comparison between your edits to the Smart Controls and the saved Smart Control settings to hear how your changes affect the sound.

▶ **EQ button**—Opens the EQ (Equalizer) effect for the selected track.

▶ **Amp and pedal buttons**—Open the Amp Designer and Pedalboard plug-ins for electric guitar audio tracks.

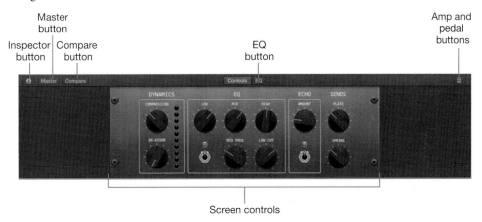

For this exercise, you'll work with the Reverb Send control in the Smart Controls inspector.

1 Click the Smart Controls inspector button (i) in the upper-left corner of the Smart Controls pane.

The Smart Controls inspector appears on the left side of the pane. Because this is an audio track, most of the controls in the inspector involve recording controls for the track.

At the bottom of the inspector you'll see the Echo Send and Reverb Send controls.

2   Make sure the audio track with the Horns region is still selected and that the cycle area is still on. Start playback.

3   Click the Reverb Send knob and drag upward until it points to the 3 o'clock position. You should be able to hear the reverb, which gives the horns a more distant but resonating sound.

4   For fun, and to annoy anyone listening to your project including yourself, drag the Echo Send control to about the same position. Okay, so maybe echo isn't for this track or this song.

5   Option-click the Echo Send control to reset it to the default position.

TIP ▶ You can Option-click any audio control to reset it to the default position. This includes the volume and pan controls in the track headers.

6   Press the Up Arrow key once to select the track above the Classic Vocal (horns) track. The Smart Controls pane updates to show controls for the selected track.

7   Press the Up Arrow key again to select the Strings Ensemble track. The Smart Controls pane now reflects the controls for that type of track.

8 Press B, or click the Smart Controls button, to hide the Smart Controls pane.

9 Press C to turn off Cycle mode.

> **NOTE** ▶ The Up Arrow and Down Arrow keys select the next higher, or lower, track.

Mission accomplished. The unnamed audio track containing the Horns region now has a reverb effect to enhance the sound. The horns part is a bit too loud at the moment, but you'll fix that at the end of the lesson when you give the track a proper name and icon. The next stop on this interface tour is the editors.

Exploring the Editors

There are four editors based on the type of track instrument: Audio Editor (for Audio tracks with audio regions), Piano Roll Editor and Score Editor (both for Software Instrument regions), and finally the Drummer Editor (for drummer tracks). You'll work with the Drummer Editor in the next lesson. For this exercise, you'll focus on the other editors.

To display an editor, you can click the Editors button, press E, or double-click a region in the timeline. For this exercise you'll use the manual double-click method. Since you've been working with the Horns region, let's go ahead and open it in the Audio Editor.

> **NOTE** ▶ If you didn't complete all of the previous exercises in this lesson, open the project (**1-2 Cycle and Horns** and save it to your projects folder on the desktop. If you have been following along, please continue working with the same project you've been using **1-1 Scales Starting**.)

1 Double-click the Horns region in the Classic Vocal track to open the Audio Editor.

Now you can clearly see the audio waveforms in the Horns region. Notice that the Real Instrument region in the Audio Editor is also blue to indicate the type of instrument region. Though the editor is a separate area of the window, it includes a ruler with a playhead and a cycle area that correspond to the same elements in the timeline.

Let's expand the waveform even further with the horizontal zoom slider. You'll want to move the playhead over the waveform first so you don't zoom in to an empty space in the region. You'll find the horizontal zoom slider in the top-right corner of the Audio Editor.

2   In the editor, drag the playhead until it is over the center of the first waveform in the Horns region. Then drag the horizontal zoom slider in the editor toward the right until the audio waveform fills the editor.

NOTE ▶ Swipe your trackpad or mouse left or right over a region in the editor to show a different portion.

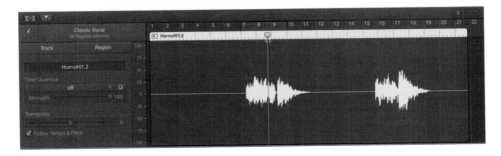

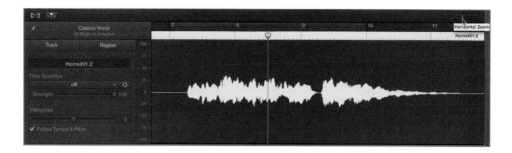

Now that you've seen a Real Instrument region in the Audio Editor, let's take a look at a Software Instrument region in the Piano Roll and Score Editors.

3   In the timeline, click the Grand Piano region in the Piano Beginning track. The region appears in the Piano Roll Editor. Swipe your track pad or mouse up or down over the Piano Roll editor to show notes played at higher or lower octaves.

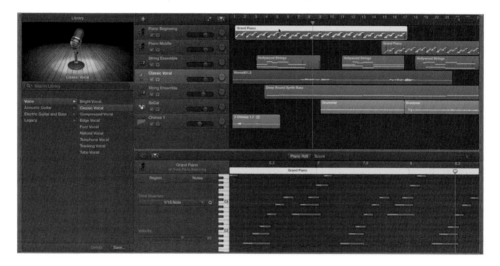

MIDI note events appear as dashes on a grid in the Piano Roll view. Each horizontal line of the grid represents a white or black note on the corresponding keyboard.

4   Click the Score button at the top of the Piano Roll Editor to change to the Score (Musical Notation) Editor.

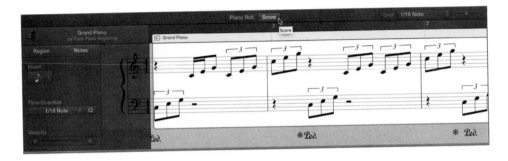

5   Drag the horizontal zoom slider in the editor right and left to see a few larger notes or the score for the entire region.

> **TIP** Whether you are in Piano Roll or Score view, you can click and hold a note in the editor to hear the note and see an overlay with the name of the note. This is useful in orchestrating additional musical parts based on Software Instrument regions. It is also great for learning musical notation. Be careful not to move the note or you will change its pitch (which note is played).

Whichever editor you use to modify Software Instrument regions you have the option of Piano Roll or Score as well as modifying an entire region or individual notes. Oh, and you can print your score as well! With GarageBand you can compose and orchestrate a musical masterpiece and never have to worry about writing down the notation. Speaking of notation, wouldn't it be great if GarageBand included a built-in note pad?

Showing the Project Note Pad

A musician's workshop/recording studio would not be complete without a note pad to jot down ideas and notes to yourself—or others—as you create. GarageBand includes a handy onscreen note pad for each project.

1   Choose View > Note Pad, press Command-Option-P, or click the Note Pad button (which looks like a pad of paper and a pencil) in the far-right side of the toolbar.

The Note Pad is a long gray area that fills the right side of the GarageBand window. You can change the font, size, and color of the text using the Control Fonts button in the upper-left corner of the Note Pad.

NOTE ▸ For this project, I used the Note Pad to keep a breakdown of which chords/notes are played during which measures (bars). This type of guide is handy for orchestrating a piece.

2   Play the project. As the project plays you can see the regions in the Tracks area, the written notes in the Note Pad, as well as the notation for the selected track in the Score Editor. Don't forget the Track Instrument patch and track icon that you can see or change in the Library.

Now that's a music workshop! Then again, sometimes less is more, especially when all you really need to see at the moment is the Tracks area and toolbar.

Project Tasks

Before you move on to the last section of this lesson, let's review some of the things you've already learned. Your goals in this exercise are to simplify the window by hiding the Library, editors, and Note Pad. Then turn on Cycle mode and create a cycle area between bar 1 and bar 11. If you feel confident in doing these things, go ahead without instruction. If you need help, here are a few hints:

1   Click the Library button or press Y to hide the Library.

2   Click the Editors button or press E to hide the Score Editor.

3   Click the Note Pad button or press Command-Option-P to hide the Note Pad.

4   Click the Cycle button or press C to turn on Cycle mode.

5   Drag the cycle area of the ruler from bar 1 to bar 11.

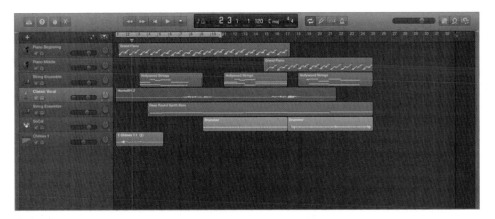

Well done. Now you are ready to move on to the last section and explore the loop browser.

NOTE ▸ If you didn't complete the project tasks, or any of the previous exercises, please open the project **1-3 Scales Tasks** to jump in to the lesson at this point.

Working with Apple Loops

Loops—musical parts that can be looped over and over to build a song—are foundational elements of GarageBand. In fact, GarageBand includes 2000 professional-quality Apple Loops.

Apple Loops are prerecorded music files that can be used to add drum beats, rhythm elements, and other repeating musical parts to a project. Loops contain musical patterns that can be repeated seamlessly and combined into new musical arrangements. You can extend a loop to fill any length of time in a project. These loops can be accessed in the loop browser.

In the next series of exercises, you'll audition tambourine loops with the song and add one to the project to create a new track. You'll then add a new percussion part near the beginning of the song.

> **NOTE ▶** If this is the first time that you have used the loop browser in GarageBand, you may be prompted to download the additional Apple Loops and instruments. This may take a few minutes. If you would like to skip the download, you can move ahead to the next lesson. Otherwise, follow the download prompt when it appears.

1   Start playback and listen to the first 10 measures (bars) of the song. Make sure you have Cycle mode turned on.

    The song works okay, but it feels like it could use a hint of percussion—perhaps a tambourine part—somewhere around the fifth or sixth measure.

    It's always nice for a song to build gradually. So a light percussion part before the drummer part kicks in around the ninth measure should work well.

    Don't worry if you don't have a tambourine and microphone handy. For this project, an Apple Loop will do the trick.

2   Choose View > Show Apple Loops, Press O, or click the Apple Loops button (which looks like a loop) on the far right side of the toolbar. The loop browser opens on the right side of the window, in the same area that the Note Pad used to be.

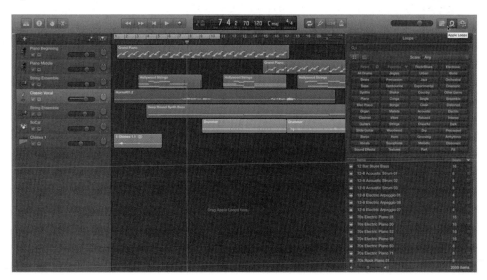

The top of the loop browser includes a search field and keyword buttons for sorting through the loops to find ones that work for your project. The lower half of the browser shows the results list based on how the loops were sorted. For this exercise you're looking for a tambourine part; there happens to be a Tambourine button, so that makes the search a click away.

3   In the loop browser, click the Tambourine button to narrow your choices from thousands of Apple Loops to 10.

4   Click the first Apple Loop in the list, Tambourine 01, to preview it.

5   Press the Down Arrow to preview the next loop in the list. Feel free to continue previewing the remaining tambourine loops.

6   Click the selected Apple Loop in the list to stop the preview.

So now you've found the tambourine parts. The next step is to audition them with the song to see which fits best.

> **NOTE** ▶ There are two types of Apple Loops: Audio loops (blue) and Software Instrument loops (green). The color of a loop's icon indicates which type of loop it is.

Auditioning and Adding Loops to the Project

To audition (play) an Apple Loop along with the project, you first need to start playback of the project. Then you click the loop you would like to hear in the loop browser to hear them at the same time—in musical time.

1   Click the Play button in the toolbar, or click the workspace and then press the Spacebar to begin playback of the cycle area.

2   Click the Tambourine 01 Apple Loop in the list to audition it. There may be a hesitation before it starts as it waits to come in at the beginning of a measure to match musical time. This one sounds too busy. Next.

3   Audition the remaining tambourine loops to find which one you like best with this song. What do you think? For me, Tambourine 04 works best because it isn't too distracting and fits well with the drummer region that starts at bar 9.

4   Click the Stop button in the toolbar to stop playback and the audition.

> **NOTE** ▶ The transport controls and shortcuts for playback work only if the workspace is selected. You can tell which area of the interfaces is selected because it will have a thin blue outline around the edges. To select an area of the interface, click inside that area.

To add a loop to the project, you can drag a loop to an existing track with the same type of instrument, or you can drag a loop to the empty space below the tracks. By dragging the loop below the existing tracks, you'll automatically create a new track named after the loop instrument. Let's try it.

5   Drag the Tambourine 04 loop from the loop browser to the empty space below the Chimes track in the timeline. Place the loop so that it starts at the beginning of bar 4. The handy position guide overlay will guide you as you move your loop into position (4 1 1). The numbers indicated by the position guide overlay correspond with the ruler and the musical time in the LCD display: bar (4) beat (1) division (1) tick (1). In most cases you'll just need to pay attention to the bar (measure) and beat.

A new Tambourine 04 track appears in the Tracks area containing the loop you just added with the same name.

6   Click the Tambourine button in the loop browser to deselect it and clear the search. Then, click the Loop Browser button to hide the browser.

7   Play the cycle area and listen to the song with the new loop. It sounds great, except that it ends too early so there is an abrupt gap in the percussion between the tambourine part and the incoming Drummer section.

NOTE ▶ Feel free to drag the horizontal zoom slider in the upper-right corner of the Tracks area to zoom in or out of the timeline as needed.

8   Click the tambourine region in the timeline to select it, if it is not already selected. Move your pointer to the top-right edge of the region. The pointer becomes the Loop tool. With the Loop tool you can extend a loop so that it repeats for a longer period of time. Notches indicate each time a loop repeats.

9   With the Loop tool, drag the right edge of the loop to the beginning of bar 10.

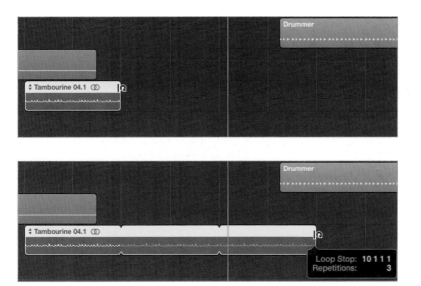

10 Press C to turn off Cycle mode and play the project one last time to hear it with the tambourine track.

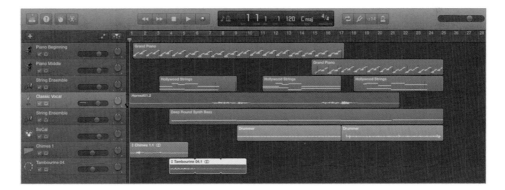

The tambourine Apple Loop works great. Trouble is, it is a little loud in the mix. Let's take a moment to turn down the tambourine and horn tracks.

Adjusting a Track's Volume

Each track header contains a Volume slider that can be used to lower the volume of the track. Mixing and balancing the volume levels between tracks is an important part of finishing a song. You'll learn much more about mixing in Lesson 8, "Mixing Music and Adding

EQ Effects." For now, you just need to know how to adjust a single track's volume level if it is distracting while you build your song.

1   In the Tambourine 04 track header, drag the Volume slider to the left to −16.0 dB.

This is significantly lower than the original volume but still loud enough to be a subtle percussive accent, instead of sounding like an annoying backup percussionist trying to outshine the other musicians.

2   Play the beginning of the song to hear the lower tambourine part. Much better, but it could use a fade-in. You'll learn how to do that in Lesson 8 as well.

3   Lower the volume level of the Classic Vocal (horns) track to −9.0 dB. Play the horns section of the song to hear the difference.

Again, a huge improvement. Finally, a lovely distant but regal-sounding horn solo that adds depth and beauty to this simple scales project.

Changing a Track's Name and Icon

Before you save and close this project and move on to the next lesson, let's fix the Classic Vocal track header so that the name and icon match the instrument part within the track. These may seem like insignificant details now, but labeling tracks is like labeling audio tapes and loose CDs. Taking the time to do it now is much easier than wasting hours down the road trying to organize your projects—especially in front of clients.

1   Double-click the track name (Classic Vocal) to open the track name field.

2   Type *Horns*, and press Return. The name of the track changes to Horns.

Track icons match the icons for the selected patch for that track by default. You can change the icon for a track any time using the icon shortcut menu.

3   Control-click (or right-click) the icon (microphone) on the Horns track header.

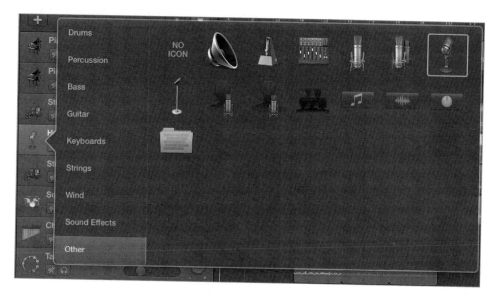

The icon shortcut menu appears.

4   From the shortcut menu, choose Wind, and then select the trumpet icon.

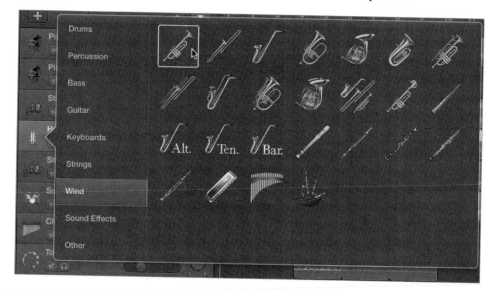

The shortcut menu closes automatically after you select a new icon. Finally, we have a horns track with a useful name and icon.

5   Choose File > Save, or press Command-S to save your progress.

Bravo! You completed the lesson and learned your way around the interface.

NOTE ▶ If you didn't complete the project tasks, or any of the previous exercises, please open the project **1-4 Scales Finished** to hear the project with the new tambourine track.

Lesson Review

1.   You can find the transport controls for playing a project in which area of the Garage-Band window?

2.   What is the difference between tracks and regions?

3.   What are the four types of musical tracks represented by different-colored regions?

4.   Which area of the GarageBand window contains the patches for changing a track's instrument?

5.   Where can you find Apple Loops to audition and add to a project?

6.   Which part of the interface allows you to change the name, volume level, and icon for a track?

Answers

1. The transport controls are in the toolbar at the top of the GarageBand window.

2. Tracks are the horizontal lanes in the tracks area that contain individual musical parts (regions). Each track is a separate instrument sound. The regions are the individual musical parts—building blocks within a track.

3. The four different types of musical tracks are Software Instrument (green), Real Instrument (blue), Real Instrument Guitar or Bass (purple), and Imported audio file (orange).

4. You can change track instruments in the Library.

5. Apple Loops are located in the loop browser.

6. You can change all of these things in the track's header. The Volume slider adjusts the track's volume. Control-click the track's icon to access the Track Icon menu. Double-click the track name to show the Name field and change the track's name.

2

Lesson Files

Time
This lesson takes approximately 60 minutes to complete.

Goals
Understanding tracks

Working with the track header controls

Creating new tracks

Duplicating tracks and regions

Renaming arrangement track markers

Creating a drummer track

Reordering tracks

Working with the Drummer Editor

Working with the movie track

Working with Tracks

In this lesson, you'll learn how to work with a variety of tracks, including Software Instrument tracks, movie tracks, arrangement tracks, and the brand-new and powerful drummer tracks. Sure, that doesn't sound like much fun—until you get a better perspective on the power of tracks. Have you ever heard of a four-track recorder? In its time, the four-track revolutionized the music industry as much as the mouse revolutionized computers. The four-track recorder made it possible to record four different instrument tracks on the same piece of tape at a time, and then play them back all mixed together. Eventually, four-track recorders were replaced by eight-track recorders, and finally by digital recording.

What does that mean to you? For one thing, you don't have to limit your songs to four tracks. In fact, depending on your computer's speed and power, you can have up to 255 Real Instrument tracks or 64 Software Instrument tracks. Chances are, most of your songs can be arranged in 10 or fewer tracks, but it's nice to know that if you need more tracks, they're there for you.

This lesson focuses on some of the different types of tracks. You'll add and duplicate tracks to build a song and even work with a virtual session drummer to create a drummer track. Finally you'll work with the arrangement track to identify the parts of the song and add a movie track.

Understanding Tracks

Think of the tracks in your timeline as the different musicians in your band. Each musician plays a different instrument and is represented by a separate track. As the leader of your band, you can decide which instruments are used in a song and how you want to record them. If you don't like an instrument part, you can always fire the musician—or in this case, just delete the track. If you really like the way a part sounds, you can clone the musician, or just double that track in the timeline.

The best way to understand tracks is to work with them, so let's get started.

Previewing the Finished Project

Most music creation follows a standard workflow: record parts, orchestrate/arrange more parts, edit/fix the recorded parts, mix the tracks, add effects, and output the finished piece. You'll notice the lessons in this book follow a similar flow.

So, before we start working with tracks and building the project for this lesson, let's fast-forward to the end and preview the finished piece. There's nothing like a good before-and-after comparison to recognize the benefits of crafty track manipulation.

1   Open the project **2-6 Ditty Finished** from the Lesson 2 folder. There's no need to save this version since you won't be making any changes.

If you look closely you'll see the arrangement track just below the ruler that shows the three parts of the song (Intro, Verse, and Chorus). Because this lesson is about working with tracks in GarageBand, it seems only fitting to include a new type of track. Another type of track is the movie track, which you will add to the project at the end of this lesson.

2   Press Return to move the playhead to the beginning of the project. Press the Spacebar to play the project.

This song isn't a masterpiece; it's not even a full song. It's more of a ditty that came to me while I was walking my dog Lexie. In fact, as I pondered over what kinds of exercises I should include in this book it occurred to me that one of the early projects should be as easy and carefree as walking my dog. So I recorded the melody Acoustic Guitar part on my iPhone with GarageBand for iOS and the Smart Guitar instrument—while walking the dog. Really! Smart Instruments in GarageBand for iOS, like Software Instruments with Smart Controls and the Arpeggiator in GarageBand for Mac, can make Software Instruments practically play themselves.

MORE INFO ▶ To learn more about GarageBand for iOS, and how it was used to create this song, you can read Bonus Lesson 2, "Working with GarageBand for iOS." You can find the bonus lesson online on the same page as the lesson files.

3   Take a look at the number of audio tracks in this project. You should see six total.

4   Play the project again. This time listen carefully to the melody (everything but the bass and drums in this piece).

The parts are identical; they're just played by different instruments. Technically, they were only played once: by my index finger on my iPhone. The point is that one part was duplicated into different tracks with different instrument sounds to enhance the music.

Now that you've heard and seen the finished project, think about this: the entire project was recorded without any musical instruments. The only tools were an iPhone, trackpad, and computer keyboard. With that in mind, let's open the starting version and get to work building tracks.

Opening a Project from GarageBand

Instead of closing the current project, then going to the Finder or Desktop, for this exercise you'll just open the lesson project from within GarageBand. Opening a project while another is open will automatically close the current project. Only one project can be open at a time in GarageBand.

1   Choose File > Open, or press Command-O to display the Open dialog.

2   In the Open dialog, select the Desktop > APTS GarageBand Book Files > Lesson 2 > **2-1 Ditty Starting**.

3   Click Open, or double-click the file **2-1 Ditty Starting** to open it.

4   If prompted to save changes to **2-6 Ditty Finished**, click Don't Save.

The project opens in the GarageBand window. Don't forget to save a version to your projects folder on the desktop.

5   Choose File > Save As to open the Save dialog.

6   In the Save dialog, select Desktop > My GarageBand Projects. Click Save.

> **NOTE** ▶ If you didn't create a My GarageBand Projects folder in Lesson 1, take a moment and create one now. That way you will have a place to save your working versions of each project.

In subsequent lessons, you will be asked to open a specific file and save it to your projects folder on the desktop.

Exploring the Starting Project

The project **2-1 Ditty Starting** has only three Software Instrument tracks: Acoustic Guitar, Fingerstyle Bass, and Fingerstyle Bass Arpeggiator.

If you look closely at the names of the regions in the Acoustic Guitar track, you'll see they are named Part A iOS Smart Guitar, Part B iOS Smart Guitar, and Part C iOS Smart Guitar. The "A," "B," and "C" reflect the default naming convention in GarageBand for iOS. I added "iOS Smart Guitar" to the name so you'd know at a glance how the part was recorded.

The Acoustic Guitar track was recorded on my iPhone with GarageBand for iOS Smart Guitar with Autoplay turned on and set to display chord strips. Parts A, B, and C each used a different Autoplay setting.

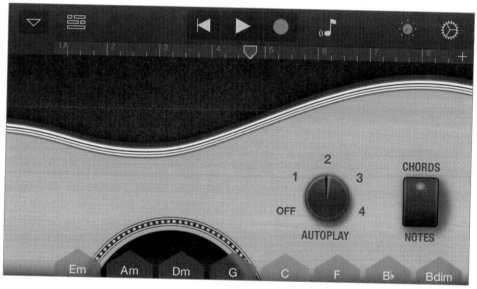

GarageBand for iOS Smart Guitar with Autoplay

1   Play the project to hear the basic tracks.

2   Play the project again and focus your attention on the bass parts.

The Fingerstyle Bass tracks were both recorded in GarageBand with Musical Typing on my computer keyboard. The difference between them is that in the first Fingerstyle Bass track I played each note as it was recorded, whereas I recorded the Fingerstyle Bass Arpeggiator track with the Arpeggiator Smart Control turned on so it played a sequence of notes for each note (key) I pressed on the computer keyboard. You'll record both of these bass parts in Lesson 4, "Recording and Editing Software Instruments."

Working with Solo and Mute Controls

With only three tracks and two types of instruments playing at a time, you probably didn't have any trouble distinguishing among the different tracks as you listened. However, as you build tracks and add instrument parts, it's a good idea to know how to solo and mute tracks as you work to allow you to focus your ears on the tracks you want to hear (or not hear) during playback.

The basic controls included in the track header are the Mute button, Solo button, Volume slider, and Pan knob. You'll work with each of these controls throughout this book. For now, you'll just use the Solo and Mute buttons.

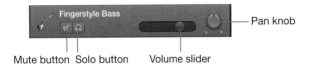

Mute button Solo button   Volume slider

NOTE ▸ Additional header controls are available through the Track menu, or the track header shortcut menu.

1   Select the Fingerstyle Bass track header; then click the Solo button (headphones) to solo that track. The Fingerstyle Bass track brightens whereas all the other tracks lose the color in their regions. This indicates they will not be heard during playback.

2   Play the soloed Fingerstyle Bass part to hear it. During playback, press S to unsolo the track and hear it with the other instruments.

The keyboard shortcut for solo is S, and the keyboard shortcut for mute is M. These shortcuts work only on the selected track or tracks.

3   Stop playback. Click the Mute buttons on both of the Bass tracks. Play the project and listen to the Acoustic Guitar track without the bass parts. When you are finished, stop playback.

Now you know how to listen to only the tracks you want during playback.

NOTE ▶ The onscreen music keyboard works only for Software Instrument tracks. GarageBand also includes a Musical Typing window that can turn your computer keyboard into a MIDI instrument. For this lesson, however, you'll just focus on the onscreen music keyboard.

2   Click any of the keys on the onscreen music keyboard to hear the notes. You can drag across the keys to play several notes in succession.

It works! But the keys are so tiny they require both patience and dexterity to play anything specific. Let's expand the keyboard and the keys at the same time.

3   Drag the lower-right corner of the keyboard down and to the right to resize it for larger keys that are easier to click.

NOTE ▶ The onscreen music keyboard is touch sensitive. Click the top of the keys to play with a lighter velocity and get a quieter sound. Click the bottom of the keys to play with a harder velocity and get a louder sound. You can always change the velocity of Software Instrument notes in the editor after they've been recorded. The blue section of the mini-keyboard above the notes shows which range of notes (octave) you are playing. You can drag the blue region right or left to change octaves in the onscreen music keyboard.

4   Play the onscreen keyboard by clicking the notes on the keyboard.

Although you can play music this way, it's not the easiest way to create complex music arrangements. However, it will work perfectly for testing the sound of a Software Instrument track.

5   Click the Acoustic Guitar track header to select that track. The onscreen music keyboard header changes to show the name of the selected track.

6   Play the onscreen keyboard to hear the Acoustic Guitar sound.

7   Select the Classic Electric Piano track header. The onscreen music keyboard changes accordingly.

Let's change the track instrument to strings, which will work better for this project.

8   In the Library, choose Orchestral > Strings > String Ensemble.

 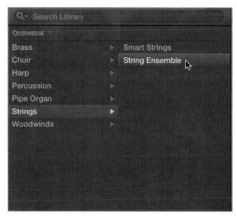

9   Click a few notes to hear the String Ensemble instrument in action.

10 Click the red close button in the upper-left corner of the onscreen keyboard to hide it.

Sounds awesome! The quality of the Software Instrument sounds in GarageBand is amazing. Now all you have to do is find loops that might work, or hire some musicians and orchestrate and record a part to go with the song. Or… you could cheat and try the guitar part in the strings track.

Moving Regions to Different Tracks

You can move regions from one track to another as long as the tracks are the same type (Software Instrument or audio track). In this exercise you'll move the first guitar region in the Acoustic Guitar track down to the new String Ensemble track to hear how it sounds.

1   Drag the Part A iOS Smart Guitar region from the Acoustic Guitar track to the String Ensemble track. Alignment guides show the position of the region as you move it. You will continue to see the selected region in its original position until you release it in the new position or track in the tracks area.

TIP ▶ Holding Shift while dragging a region from one track to another constrains the horizontal movement so that the region stays in the same position in the timeline as you move it vertically from track to track. Just be sure to select the region and start to move it before you press Shift. Otherwise, if you press Shift first, you will not be able to drag the region at all.

2   Play the first part of the song. What do you think of the new strings part? A little busy, but it will work for now. You'll learn how to clean it up in Lesson 4.

3   Choose Edit > Undo Drag, or press Command-Z to undo the maneuver.

4   Close the Library so you'll have more room in the tracks area to work.

Why did you undo your last move? Because rather than moving just one region, you're going to duplicate them all and move the duplicates to the new track all at the same time. Besides, just like music, practice makes perfect.

Duplicating Regions with Option-Drag

Regions can be edited within tracks similar to words in a word processor. You can cut, copy and paste, delete, and duplicate regions in the Edit menu, or by using keyboard shortcuts. For this exercise you'll use Option-drag to create duplicate regions and move them at the same time.

To begin, simply select a region or regions in a track and hold down the Option key while dragging; this creates a duplicate region. Be careful not to release the Option key before you release the duplicate regions or you will simply move the original regions.

1   Select the Acoustic Guitar track header. All three regions in the track become selected.

2   Option-drag the selected guitar regions and drop the duplicate regions in the String Ensemble track, directly below the Acoustic Guitar track. A green plus (+) indicates you are adding new regions (duplicating) rather than just moving regions.

3   Play the project to hear the two tracks together. Nice, but the strings seem a little overpowering. That can easily be remedied by turning down the volume of the String Ensemble track.

4   Drag the Volume slider on the String Ensemble track toward the left to −6.0 dB. Now it will play 6 decibels (dB) quieter than the default level (loudness) 0.0 dB.

5   Play the beginning of the project. Notice the difference with the strings part now that it is lower in volume.

6   Press Command-S to save your progress.

    If you did not complete the previous exercises, open the project 2-2 Strings Added and save it to your folder on the desktop.

As you can see—and hear—duplicating regions and assigning different instruments is a simple yet effective way to build tracks to enhance a song.

Zooming In and Out of the Timeline

Before you make any other changes to the new String Ensemble track, this is a good time to use the horizontal zoom slider in the tracks area menu bar to get a better look at the first part of the song. The keyboard shortcuts for zooming in and out of the timeline are, respectively, Command-Right Arrow and Command-Left Arrow.

1   Move the playhead to the beginning of the song.

2   Press Command-Right Arrow or drag the horizontal zoom slider toward the right until you only see the first 9 to 12 measures (bars) in the ruler.

This way, the entire visible tracks area is dedicated to the first part of the song.

Resizing Regions in the Tracks Area

There is just one last step to complete the strings part in this lesson, and that is to resize the first region so that it starts later in the song. One of the secrets of creating music is to let the songs build rather than have all the instrument parts start at once. Resizing the first region in the String Ensemble track so that it starts later will give the acoustic impression that the string ensemble joins the guitarist in the song.

For this exercise, your goal is to resize the region so that it begins at bar 5. To do so, you will need to trim the left edge of the region.

1   Hover the pointer over the lower-left corner of the first region in the String Ensemble track (Part A iOS Smart Guitar). The pointer changes to the Resize/Trim tool (left-right pointing arrows).

2   Drag the lower-left corner of the region to the beginning of bar 5 (5 1 1 1). As you resize the region, it will remain intact until you release the Resize/Trim tool.

3   If needed, click the empty tracks area to deselect the region. Play the beginning of the song to hear the changes. What a difference it makes to have musical parts come in at different times!

4   Press Return to move the playhead to the beginning of the song. Press Command-Left Arrow, or drag the horizontal zoom slider toward the left to see the entire song in the timeline.

This little ditty is starting to sound more like a song. Let's treat it that way and give each section a proper musical name.

Working with the Arrangement Track

Most songs are arranged in distinct sections such as introduction, verse, and chorus. The arrangement track—which appears below the time ruler—makes it easy to see these parts of your song and to move, duplicate, or delete those sections at any time. You'll work with moving the sections around in Lesson 4, "Recording and Editing Software Instruments." For now you'll display the arrangement track and change the names of each section of the song.

1   Choose Track > Show Arrangement Track. The arrangement track appears in the timeline below the ruler. This track includes three arrangement markers, each labeling a section of the song.

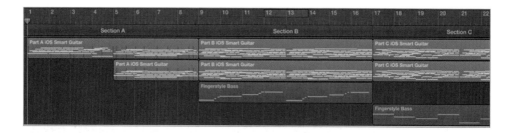

The arrangement track for this project follows the naming convention of the musical parts that were recorded in GarageBand for iOS and shared via iCloud.

Let's change the names of the arrangement markers to match the musical parts of this song (Intro, Verse, Chorus).

2   Hover over the name of the first arrangement marker until you see a shortcut menu icon (opposing arrows pointing up and down). Click the shortcut menu and choose Intro.

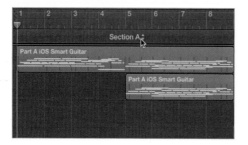 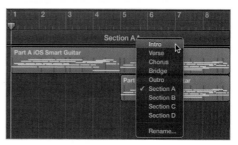

The arrangement marker is now named Intro for the introduction of the song.

NOTE ▶ When you select an arrangement marker, it brightens. Once selected, all musical parts in that section of the timeline can be inadvertently deleted. So it's a good idea to deselect arrangement markers when you aren't using them. To deselect, click any empty space in the tracks area.

3   Change the name of the Section B arrangement marker to *Verse*.

4   Change the name of the Section C arrangement marker to *Chorus*.

5   If necessary, click the empty space in the tracks area to deselect the arrangement markers. Save your work.

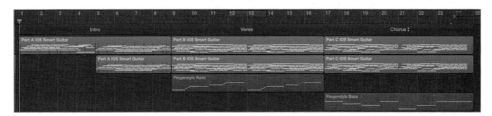

Now that the sections of the song have proper musical names, the remaining exercises in this lesson will refer to these sections by their new names.

Duplicating a Track

Earlier in the lesson you created a new track and added duplicate guitar regions to make a strings part. For this exercise, you'll duplicate the Acoustic Guitar track and drag copies of the parts to the duplicate track. In Lesson 8 you'll add an EQ effect to make the doubled track sound like a different guitar. Doubling tracks like this is a sure way to "fatten" the sound and make a particular musical line stand out. In this case, instead of it sounding like one guitar player, it will sound like two who practice quite a bit, because they play together in perfect unison.

1   If you didn't complete the previous exercises, open the project **2-3 With Markers** and save it to your folder.

2   Select the Acoustic Guitar track header.

> **TIP** ▶ You can press the Up Arrow and Down Arrow keys to change which track is selected (Up Arrow selects the track above, and Down Arrow selects the track below).

3   Choose Track > New Track With Duplicate Settings, or press Command-D to duplicate the selected track. A duplicate Acoustic Guitar track appears directly below the selected track.

Creating a new track with duplicate settings makes a new track, but it does not include any regions. No problem. You already know how to do that.

Project Tasks

It's time to review and practice some of the skills you've already learned in this lesson. Your goal is to select all of the regions in the first Acoustic Guitar track and Option-drag them to the new Acoustic Guitar track. Once the regions are in place, open the Library for the new Acoustic Guitar track. Mute the String Ensemble track so that you only hear the guitar tracks. If you have the full install of all the GarageBand sounds, try all of the different guitar patches during playback. If you are using the free install, try the Classic Clean guitar sound. When you are finished with the guitar patch trials, choose the Acoustic Guitar patch. Turn off the mute buttons for all tracks and listen to the Intro Verse and Chorus. Finally, save your work. If you are confident in following the above directions, go for it. If you prefer a little more guidance, here are some basic steps.

1   Click the top Acoustic Guitar track header to select all the regions.

2   Option-drag the regions to the new Acoustic Guitar track.

3   Double-click the new Acoustic Guitar track header to show the Library for that track.

4   Mute the String Ensemble track.

5   Start playback. In the Library, select a different Guitar patch.

6   Continue playback while you click each of the different guitar sounds to change the patch for the selected track. You can also use the Up or Down Arrow keys to select the next sound accordingly.

7   Select the Acoustic Guitar patch if it is not already selected.

8   Option-click one of the active (blue) Mute buttons to un-mute all of the muted tracks. Listen to the song with the doubled guitar part.

9   Hide the Library and save your work.

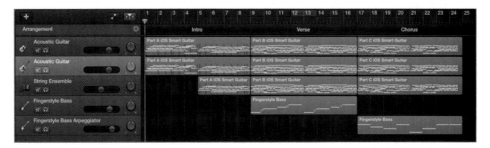

Voilà! You created a second acoustic guitar part without recording a new one. Now all this song needs is a drummer.

> **NOTE ▶** If you didn't complete the previous exercises, open the project **2-4 Doubled Guitar** and save it to your folder.

Creating a Drummer Track

GarageBand has always made it easy for musicians and composers of all skill levels to create music. However, up until now creating realistic-sounding drum tracks has been a challenge for those of us who don't play drums. Sure, there are pre-recorded Apple loops and drum machine patterns you can record, but in both cases the repetitive nature of the tracks have a tendency to sound like digitally created patterns rather than performances.

But wait, there's more! You are about to experience one of the coolest and most intuitive GarageBand enhancements ever—something so amazing it allows you to instantly create human-sounding drum tracks.

That's right. GarageBand now features Drummer, your own virtual session drummer who follows along with your song, takes directions, and never misses a beat.

1   Choose Track > New Track, or click the Add Track button.

2   In the New Tracks dialog, select the drummer track. Click Create.

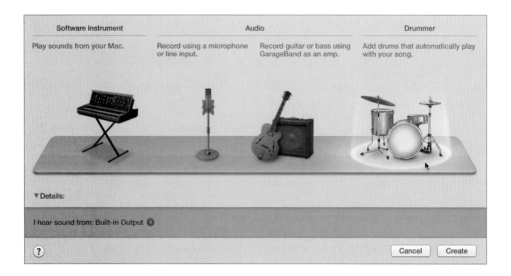

Whoa. The GarageBand window just transformed to accommodate your new virtual session drummer, Kyle.

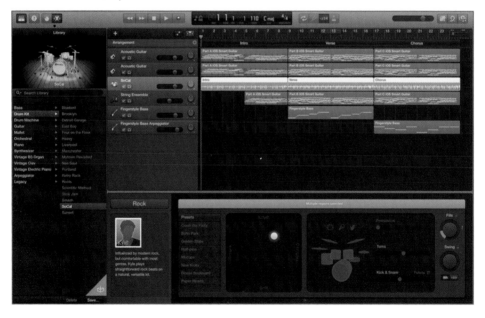

At a glance, you'll see both the Library and Drummer Editor are showing. There's also a brand-new SoCal Drummer track below whichever track you had selected. The SoCal Drummer track contains three yellow drummer regions, each with the same name as the song part indicated in the arrangement track. (It's a good thing we took care of naming the arrangement markers earlier.)

On the left side of the Drummer Editor is more information about your drummer. Kyle is a default virtual drummer with Southern California style, who plays straight-forward rock beats on a natural, versatile kit.

3   To simplify the GarageBand window, press Y or click the Library button to hide the Library. You can leave the Drummer Editor showing—just try not to click anything until the next exercise. Feel free to zoom in or out as needed to see the entire drummer track in the timeline.

4   Play the song to hear the drummer track in action. As the song plays, notice how Kyle changes things up between sections of the song to better match the music. What do you think?

Kyle rocks! And so far all you have done is add a drummer track. The drum parts sound incredible, though the drummer region in the Intro section feels too busy and intense for this song. No worries—you can simplify Kyle's drum kit and give him some direction to change the feel of the Intro section. First, let's move the drummer track to a different position in the tracks area. Since there can only be one drummer track in a project, you might as well move it where it is easiest to see.

Reordering Tracks

Chances are your SoCal track is near your Acoustic Guitar tracks. Wherever it appears in the timeline, you can easily move it by dragging the track header up or down to a new position. Your goal in this exercise is to drag the SoCal drummer track to the lowest track position so that it will be directly above the Drummer Editor. If you don't need to move your drummer track, you can skip ahead to the next section.

1   Locate the empty space in the SoCal track header. This is the best place to drag the header without inadvertently changing any track settings.

2 Drag the SoCal track header downward to the empty space below the lowest track (Fingerstyle Bass Arpeggiator). Release the track header.

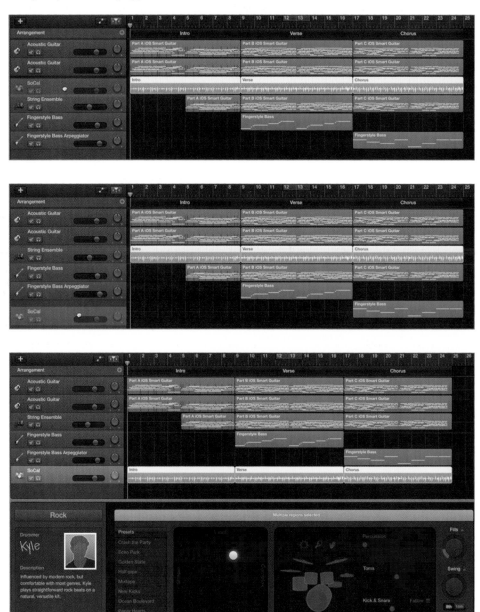

That's it. Now the drummer track is directly above the Drummer Editor.

Exploring the Drummer Editor

The Drummer Editor allows you to change drummers, use presets to choose a different playing style for your selected drummer, direct your drummer's performance, and even add or take away instruments from their drum kit.

The Drummer Editor, like other instrument editors, has controls for the entire track as well as controls for the selected drummer region. You'll find the drummer track controls—such as genres and drummers—on the left side of the Drummer Editor. Region controls—such as presets, kit variations, fill settings, and an XY pad for adjusting the loudness and complexity of the region performance—are on the right side.

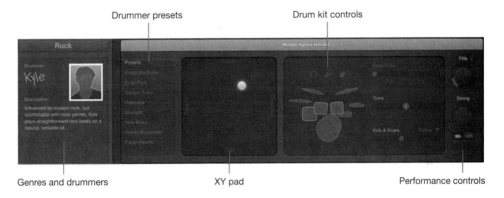

- ▶ **Genres and drummers area**—Here you can select a musical genre and choose from the various drummers available for that genre.

- ▶ **Drummer presets list**—From this list choose a preset for the selected drummer region. These presets include all the region settings located to the right of the presets list in the Drummer Editor.

- ▶ **XY pad**—This control allows you to adjust the complexity and loudness of the selected region's performance.

- ▶ **Drum kit controls**—These visual kit controls give you the power to choose different combinations of drum and percussion pieces to use in the kit.

- ▶ **Performance controls**—Use these controls to adjust the length and number of drum fills in a region. The Swing knob can vary the shuffle feel of a region. Clicking the Details button reveals additional performance controls.

Auditioning Drummer Presets

You'll work with the Drummer Editor throughout this book. For now, let's try different drummer presets to find one that works better with the Intro.

> **TIP** Always check which region or regions are selected before you start making changes in the editor.

1   Look for the name of the selected region in the yellow bar at the top of the Drummer Editor. Chances are it says "Multiple regions selected" because the drummer track regions are still selected from when you moved the track header. It also means that you can make adjustments to multiple drummer regions at the same time.

2   Click the empty space in the tracks area to deselect the drummer regions. Select the Intro region at the beginning of the drummer track. The name of the selected region is on the left side of the yellow ruler at the top of the Drummer Editor.

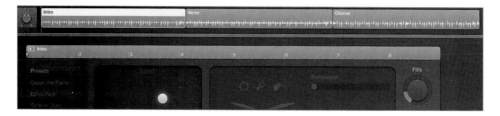

3   Play the Intro section of the song to listen to the Intro Drummer region as is.

4   In the timeline, create a cycle area over the Intro section of the song (bar 1 to bar 9). This way, playback will cycle over just that section of the song. This will make listening to different presets much easier.

In this exercise you'll display the movie track, open a movie, and resize the movie window.

> **NOTE ▶** If you didn't complete the previous exercises, open the project **2-5 Ditty Drummer** and save it to your folder.

1   Choose Track > Show Movie Track.

An empty movie track appears between the arrangement track and the first instrument track. There are several ways to open a movie file, including using the File menu or pressing Option-Command-O. For this exercise you'll use the shortcut menu in the movie track header. You'll find the movie for this project in the Additional Media folder in the APTS GarageBand Book Files folder on your desktop.

2   Click the movie track name in the header, and then choose Open Movie from shortcut menu.

3   In the Open dialog, select the **Lexie Shadow.mov** file (Desktop > APTS GarageBand Book Files > Additional Media > **Lexie Shadow.mov**). Click Open.

NOTE ▸ There can only be one movie file in the movie track. If you wish to remove the current movie file, you can choose Remove Movie from the shortcut menu in the movie track header.

Right away you'll notice a dog in the middle of your workspace. That's my dog Lexie, who was the inspiration for this ditty. Not only did I record the guitar part from my iPhone while walking her, I also made this video—though not at the same time. I watched her movement and her cadence (step pattern) when I created the melody; you judge for yourself if I managed to capture the carefree feeling. Regardless, you've added a movie, so let's watch it.

4   Play the project to see Lexie in action. Once again, it's not a masterpiece, but it works.

Although the movie file is called Lexie Shadow, the movie window is named after the project. You'll see the name of the project in the movie window header.

5   Drag the movie window header to move it to another location on the screen. Drag the edges of the movie window to resize it.

6   Click the close button (X) in the upper-left corner of the movie window to minimize it.

Where did it go? Take a look at the movie track header. The minimized movie window is now thumbnail-sized. You'll also see a new audio track called Lexie Shadow (named after the movie file) at the top of the track. The orange color indicates that it is an imported file. Notice the thumbnail strip in the movie track. These thumbnails can be used as a reference if you are scoring the video.

7   Click the minimized movie window to return it to its last size and location on the screen.

8   Play the project one last time for nostalgia's sake. When you are finished, save your work.

Congratulations! You covered a lot of tracks in this lesson. Not only did you create tracks and change track instruments, but you also named the musical parts in the arrangement track, created and edited a drummer track, and worked with the movie track. In the next lesson you'll build a project from scratch using Apple Loops. Feel free to experiment with this project, modify the drummer regions in the verse and chorus, or change track instruments.

Lesson Review

1. How can you listen to the Software Instrument sound patched to an empty Software Instrument track?

2. What are the four choices in the New Track dialog?

3. Which buttons in the interface control the tracks that are audible during playback? Where are the buttons located?

4. What keyboard shortcut can you use while dragging regions in the timeline to duplicate the selected region or regions?

5. Which area of the GarageBand window contains the patches for changing a track's instrument?

6. Where do you change the performance, presets, and other parameters of a drummer track?

7. How many movie, arrangement, and drummer tracks can you have in a GarageBand project?

Answers

1. You can use the onscreen musical keyboard to play notes and hear the Software Instrument sound patched to an empty Software Instrument track.

2. The four choices in the New Track dialog are: Software Instrument, Audio to record a microphone, Audio to record a guitar or bass using GarageBand as an amp, and Drummer.

3. The Mute and Solo buttons are located in the track header and can be used to control which tracks are audible during playback.

4. You can use the Option keyboard shortcut while dragging regions in the timeline to duplicate them.

5. The Library is the area of the GarageBand window containing patches for changing a track's instrument.

6. You can change the performance, presets, and other parameters of a drummer track in the Drummer Editor.

7. A GarageBand project can have one movie track, one arrangement track, and one drummer track.

3

Lesson Files	APTS GarageBand Book Files > Lesson 3 > 3-1 Slow Motion Loops, 3-2 Arranging Loops, 3-3 Rhythm Finished, 3-4 Loopy Ringtone Finished. APTS GarageBand Book Files > Lesson Bonus Projects > 3 Sweet Looping Finished
Time	This lesson takes approximately 60 minutes to complete.
Goals	Explore the Ringtone template
	Search for Apple Loops
	Customize keyword buttons
	Mark loops as favorites
	Arrange a ringtone using Apple Loops

Working with Apple Loops and Arranging a Song

Apple Loops are pre-recorded music files that are designed to repeat (loop) over and over seamlessly. Loops are commonly used for drum-beats, rhythm parts, and other repeating musical phrases or riffs within a song. GarageBand has a whopping 2,000 pre-recorded Apple Loops. Five hundred loops come with the free version of GarageBand 10, and you get an additional 1,500 with the onetime in-app purchase. Apple Loops are incredibly flexible instrument regions that can be arranged, trimmed, and repeated to create a song or enhance your recorded tracks.

To extend your Loop Library, you can add third-party loops as well as Apple Loops from Logic Pro. You can also save your own recordings as loops in your Loop Library. You'll record and save a loop in Lesson 7, "Creating Drum and Percussion Tracks."

In this lesson, you'll learn how to search for Apple Loops and use them to arrange a piece of music. In fact, you get to create a ringtone from scratch using only Apple Loops. As you build the project, you'll learn different search techniques and discover how adaptable loops can be to fit your project. You'll also explore some advanced music-arranging techniques.

> **NOTE ▶** I'm working with the full set of 2,000 Apple Loops, so some of my screenshots may not match what you see, and the number of loops returned for each search will differ if you are working with the free version of GarageBand 10. All of the loops needed to build this project are included in the free version.

Opening a New Project Template

The previous projects you've worked on were already in progress when you started. In this exercise you'll create a loop-based project from scratch using the Ringtone template in the Project Chooser. Once the template opens, you'll immediately save it in your desktop projects folder.

1   Open GarageBand. If GarageBand is already open, choose File > New.

2   In the Project Chooser, click the New Project button to see a list of project templates.

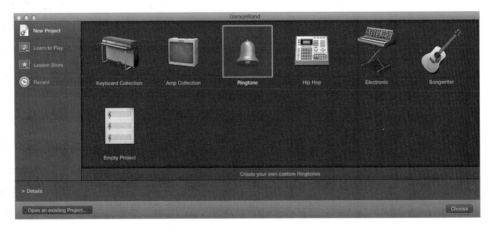

3   Double-click the Ringtone template button to automatically open the project template.

4   Save the project as *Loopy Ringtone* to your My GarageBand Projects folder.

Now that the project has been opened and saved, let's get to work.

Exploring the Ringtone Template

GarageBand templates are like having a personal assistant (or apprentice) prep the recording studio/music workshop for you before you get to work. Each project template opens with GarageBand features already turned on or showing what you'll likely need for the new project—in this case, a ringtone.

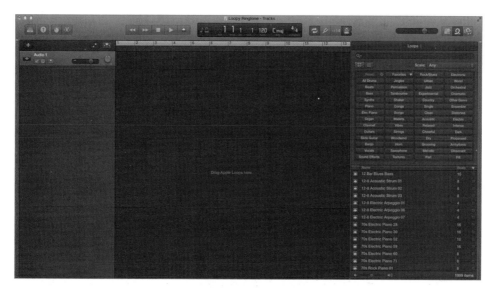

The default Ringtone template includes five handy ringtone-friendly features:

▶   **An empty Audio 1 track**—Every project needs at least one audio track. Most of the Apple Loops are audio recording (blue) regions so they can be added to the empty track.

▶ **The loop browser showing**—This makes it easy to search for Apple Loops to use in your project.

▶ **Cycle mode turned on**—As the name suggests, ringtones are a short piece of music that repeats over and over to indicate an incoming call. Therefore the music needs to sound good as it repeats, and the best way to hear that is to build and listen to it in Cycle mode. The yellow cycle area is exactly 20 bars (measures) in length, because 20 bars is nearly the limit for a ringtone in iTunes. The actual time-based limit for a ringtone is 40 seconds.

▶ **End-of-project marker set to bar 20**—This often-overlooked but useful tool indicates the project endpoint. This marker allows you to set where the song ends in the time-line. The default setting for new projects is at bar 32. However, since ringtones need to be fewer than 20 bars (or 40 seconds), the Ringtone preset took care of setting it for you.

▶ **The metronome in the toolbar is turned on (purple)**—This is so you have a click track to keep time with the project tempo.

Cycle button   Metronome button

Cycle area   End-of-project marker

Since the last three features listed may not be obvious at first glance, you can easily verify them for yourself.

1   If needed, press Command-Left Arrow/Command-Right Arrow or use the horizontal zoom slider to change the zoom level of the timeline until you see the entire cycle region. As you can see, the cycle area extends from the beginning of bar 1 to the beginning of bar 20.

   If you look carefully at bar 20 in the time ruler, you will see the end-of-project marker.

2   Start playback. You can hear the 4/4 time signature (4 clicks for each measure/bar). Follow the playhead in the ruler as you listen to the click track. Beat marks in the

ruler coincide with the audible clicks. The first beat of a measure is always at the beginning. Stop playback.

Now that you understand the features in the Ringtone template, it's time to get to work building the actual ringtone.

Understanding Loop Preferences

One housekeeping item before we start working in the loop browser is to check the Loops preferences. Plus, it is a good time to learn where these preferences are so you can find them on your own later. You'll find the GarageBand preferences in the Garage-Band menu.

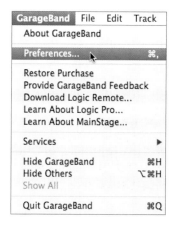

1   Choose GarageBand > Preferences. The Preferences window opens.

2   Click the Loops button at the top of the Preferences window to display the Loops preferences.

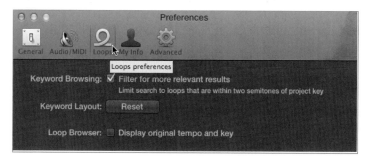

The Loops preferences include:

▶ **Keyword Browsing: Filter for more relevant results**—When this checkbox is selected, only loops in keys close to the project key appear in the loop browser.

▶ **Keyword Layout: Reset**—Clicking this button resets the keyword buttons in the loop browser back to their original positions and names.

▶ **Loop Browser: Display original tempo and key**—When this checkbox is selected, the Tempo and Key columns appear in the loop browser.

3 Keep the Loops preferences open and glance at the lower-right corner of the loop browser to see the number of loops available in your browser.

NOTE ▶ Depending on what has been installed on your Mac, the number of loops showing may differ from the screenshot.

4 Deselect the Keyword Browsing checkbox. Now your loop browser will list all of your indexed loops, not just the ones close to the project key. (If you don't know what that means, you will shortly.) Check the number of loops listed in your loop browser. Chances are the number has increased.

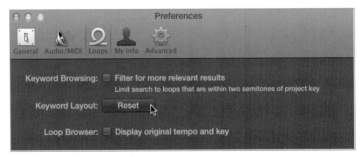

5 Click the Reset button to reset the Keyword Layout.

6 Select the "Loop Browser: Display original tempo and key" checkbox. In the results list of the loop browser you'll see the original tempo and key of each loop. When

a loop is added to the timeline, it conforms to the tempo and key of the project, as shown in the LCD display.

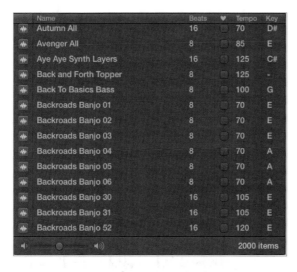

7   Deselect the "Loop Browser: Display original tempo and key" checkbox. Close the Loops preferences.

Now you are ready to search for loops to build the song.

Searching for Loops

Every song starts with an idea or inspiration, usually in the form of lyrics, rhythm, or melody. Since we have no vocal lyrics for this ringtone, the inspiration will be either rhythm- or melody-based. For this ringtone I'm hoping to find a grooving electric-sounding melody riff that can be built up with some cool beats.

As a composer, I need to hear only one catchy loop that fits the type of music I'm going for, and the rest builds from there. So for this project, you'll follow my lead.

In addition to the 2,000 loops available with GarageBand 10 and the in-app purchase, if you had previous versions of GarageBand or Logic Pro, you will have access to all those loops as well.

Where to start? Because I'm a pianist and don't have a loopy piano ringtone on my phone (yet), we are looking for a processed piano melody that will work well with electronic beats.

1   In the search field, type *piano*. Hey, what luck. The results list includes quite a few loops with Piano in the name.

Since we are looking for a loop to carry the melody, let's sort them by the number of beats to find the longest ones.

2   Click twice on the Beat column header in the results list to sort the piano loops by the number of beats with the highest number (32 beats) at the top of the list.

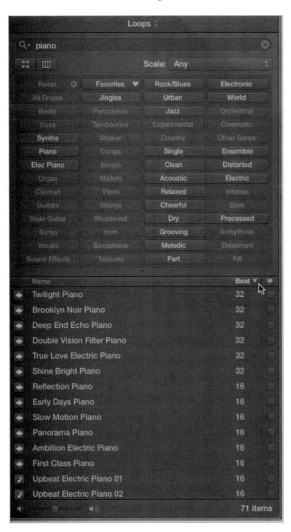

3   Click Twilight Piano in the results list to preview the loop. When you are done previewing the loop, click it again to stop. Wow! I'm inspired already. All by itself it has a grooving electric, melodic, ringtone-ish quality.

In fact, if you look at the keyword buttons, you'll see that descriptive keyword buttons for Grooving, Melodic, and Electric are bold type to indicate they apply to the current loops in the results list. Keywords that do not show any loops with the selected keyword are dimmed (inactive). You can use the active buttons to further narrow the results list if needed.

4   Drag Twilight Piano from the results list to the beginning of the Audio 1 track in the timeline.

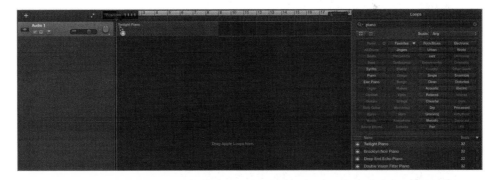

The track name changes to Twilight Piano, and the blue audio region in the timeline contains the pre-recorded Apple Loop.

NOTE ▶ If you need to move a loop to the beginning of the track, just drag the loop from the middle into position within the track.

Now that we have found the Twilight Piano, let's find some additional loops to go with it. Since the melody is rather fast-moving, a nice contrast would be to find slower-sounding loops.

5   In the search field, type *slow motion*. There are four different Slow Motion loops in the list (five if you are working with all 2,000 loops). Each loop has the same root name. That means these pieces were all composed to go together. Let's try them.

6   Preview all of the Slow Motion variations to decide if they sound like they will fit with the Twilight Piano. Sure, they sound good and feel like they'll work, but there is only one way to know for sure.

Now you have a choice to either audition the Slow Motion loop variations by previewing them while the Twilight Piano region plays in the timeline or just drag them each to a different track and evaluate them in the timeline. For this exercise, let's go with the second method and get this song going.

7   Drag Slow Motion Phaser Guitar from the loop browser to the empty space below the first track. Do the same for the Slow Motion Piano, Slow Motion Beat 01, and Slow Motion Beat 02 loops until you have all four in separate tracks in the timeline.

8   Play the loops to hear how they all sound together. Hmm. They sound like they want to work, but something is conflicting with the melody in the first half. Obviously if these loops all carry the same root name they were meant to go together. When in doubt, look for the ones that are a different length.

Beats are beats and generally go together no matter how you arrange them. So that leaves the Slow Motion Piano loop that seems to be half the length of the remaining three loops. Slow Motion Piano is only 16 beats long, whereas the other regions are all 32 beats. This song is using 4/4 time signature (as shown in the LCD display). That means there are 4 beats per bar (measure). The first beat starts at the beginning of each measure.

▶   4 beats × 8 measures = 32 beats for the longer regions.

▶   4 beats × 4 measures = 16 beats in length for the shorter piano variation.

Of course, you don't have to do the math; you can just look at the Beats column in the loop browser. Chances are the Slow Motion Piano loop was meant to go with the second half of the longer regions to add a little variation and let the song build—what a novel idea.

9   Drag the Slow Motion Piano region toward the right until it starts at bar 5 and ends at bar 9.

10 Play the project. Press K to kill the metronome (technically the metronome will be fine; that's just a term used for turning something off). And thinking of *k* for *kill* might help you remember the shortcut for turning on and off the metronome. Now this project sounds like a ringtone song.

> **NOTE ▸** The Metronome button glows purple when it is on. At any time throughout this lesson, feel free to turn the metronome on or off as needed.

11 Stop playback and save your progress.

12 In the loop browser, click the Name column header so that the results list will sort the loops alphabetically rather than by the number of beats.

You have successfully built a short musical piece with loops that will work as a ringtone. Then again, anyone can drag four like-named loops to the timeline and call it a song. Time to dive into some more advanced search and loop arrangement techniques to expand this loop inspiration into a head-bobbing, attention-getting, worthy-of-answering ringtone.

Deleting a Track

As you build a song, you will often face the decision of which tracks or loops to keep and which to delete. You could just mute tracks you aren't sure about, but over time you could have a timeline with more muted tracks than active ones. If you are unsure about a loop that you know you can always get again, just delete the track to keep things tidy in your workspace. In this exercise you'll delete the Slow Motion Beat 01 track. Keep in mind it works fine, but we're going to mix things up for the beats for this song.

> **NOTE** ▸ If you did not complete all of the previous exercises in this lesson, open the project *3-1 Slow Motion Loops* and save it to your projects folder.

1   Select the Slow Motion Beat 01 track header to select the track.

2   Press Command-Delete. A warning dialog appears to tell you that there are regions in the track. This is a helpful warning to stop you from accidentally deleting a track with recorded regions in it. In this case, you are more than willing to delete the tracks and the regions. Click OK.

There should now be only four tracks in the timeline.

Working with Keyword Buttons

In the next series of exercises you'll use keyword buttons in the loop browser to search for percussion and beats loops to enhance the current project. Using keyword buttons, you can search for loops by instrument, genre, and mood.

The first thing you need to remember to do before starting a new search in the loop browser is to always clear the search field and reset the buttons if needed.

1   Click the clear button (X) on the right side of the search field to clear the field and the results list. You won't need to reset the keyword buttons yet because you haven't used them since you reset the preferences.

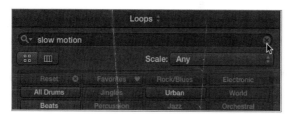

To make this ringtone stand out, there needs to be some kind of percussion at the beginning that isn't too overbearing. When in doubt, there is always the iconic first instrument nearly everyone has played at least once in their youth: the maracas.

2   Look over the keyword buttons for Maraca. Unfortunately, you won't find one, at least not yet. We'll fix that later. In addition to being an ancient multicultural rhythm-making device known the world over, the maraca is also a percussion instrument. Click the Percussion button.

You'll see a maracas loop named Big Maracas 02 in the results list.

3   Click Big Maracas 02 in the results list to hear it. Yep. Those are some grooving maracas.

4   Drag Big Maracas 02 from the loop browser to the empty space in the tracks area to create a new Big Maracas 02 track. If necessary, move the region to the beginning of the track.

5   Play the beginning of the song. Listen for the maracas sound with the other tracks.

If it is hard to hear a track, you can turn up the volume on the track header in a minute. First, it's a good idea to understand how the volume levels were determined when you created the tracks.

Adjusting Volume Levels

New tracks are normally created with the default volume level of 0.0 dB, because that is the default level for a track in which you plan to record. Tracks created by dragging loops from the loop browser automatically have their volume set to whatever level the loop browser was when you added the loop to the timeline. The default level is –6.0. Why are the defaults different? Audio is cumulative, which means the more sounds you play at the same time, the louder the overall volume becomes. The pre-recorded files in the loop browser were professionally recorded, so their levels are strong enough to stand alone or be combined. By lowering them to –6.0 dB, you have more room to lower or raise the levels when you mix. You'll learn more about mixing in Lesson 8, "Mixing Music and Adding EQ Effects."

Let's take a minute and adjust the loop browser and track mixer volume levels.

> **NOTE ▸** The correlation between the volume levels of the browser and the track created by a browser item is a real mixing timesaver if you are auditioning loops with a song. The level you set in the browser to make the loop sound good with the song will also be the level of the track the loop creates when brought into the timeline.

1 Option-click the volume slider in the loop browser to reset it to the default level (–6.0 dB).

2 Double-click the volume slider on the Twilight Piano track to show the Track Volume field. Type *-6.0* and press Return.

3 If needed, set the volume levels of the other tracks to –6.0 dB. You can either drag the volume sliders or double-click to use the Track Volume field.

4 Play the project to hear all the loops at equal volume levels.

Now that all of the tracks are the same volume level, you may have noticed that the Slow Motion Phaser Guitar region is overpowering the Twilight Piano. I like how they work together, but let's save it for the second half of the song.

5 Mute the Slow Motion Phaser Guitar track. Play the song again. Perfect—you can hear the intricate Twilight Piano and there is just enough maracas percussion to go along with the lead melody.

Now that you understand the volume levels of the tracks and loop browser, let's customize the keyword buttons.

Customizing the Keyword Buttons

Not only are keyword buttons easy to use, but they're also easy to move or swap. To move a button, all you have to do is drag the button to a different button location. The button you move will swap places with the button in the current location. The only buttons that cannot be moved are the mood buttons, Reset, and Favorites.

Why would you want to move a button? Good question. Since you know that you want certain instruments for the song, you'll want to group all the instrument buttons together near a common descriptor so you can spend less time searching for buttons and more time searching for loops.

For this song, you'll need beats with a grooving, urban sound. Let's go ahead and move those keyword buttons to the bottom row so they are all together.

1   Click the (orange) Reset button to deselect any currently selected buttons. The Reset button glows orange only if a button has been selected.

2   Locate the Beats button in the loop browser. Hint: It's in the first column, two buttons below Reset.

3   Drag the Beats button down to the bottom of the first column of buttons and release it over the Sound Effects button in the bottom row.

The Beats and Sound Effects buttons swap positions in the keyword buttons area.

4   Locate the Electronic button (at the top of the fourth column) and drag it to the bottom of the second column.

5   Locate the Grooving button (near the bottom of the third column). It happens to be a mood keyword button so it cannot be moved or changed. Luckily it is so close to the others you just moved that it is fine where it is.

NOTE ▶ Mood keyword buttons, located in the lower half of the third and fourth columns, are musical opposites and placed together so that only one or the other can be selected. If you look carefully at these mood keyword buttons you'll see that the space between them is very thin—as though they were attached to each other.

Reset ○	Favorites ♥	Rock/Blues	Textures
All Drums	Jingles	Urban	World
Sound Effects	Percussion	Jazz	Orchestral
Bass	Tambourine	Experimental	Cinematic
Synths	Shaker	Country	Other Genre
Piano	Conga	Single	Ensemble
Elec Piano	Bongo	Clean	Distorted
Organ	Mallets	Acoustic	Electric
Clavinet	Vibes	Relaxed	Intense
Guitars	Strings	Cheerful	Dark
Slide Guitar	Woodwind	Dry	Processed
Banjo	Horn	Grooving	Arrhythmic
Vocals	Saxophone	Melodic	Dissonant
Beats	Electronic	Part	Fill

All three descriptors are near each other at the bottom of the keyword buttons area (just above the results list). Just one last thing: Let's change the name of a button to an instrument that doesn't currently have a button showing: the cowbell. Country-style loops wouldn't be a good fit for this project, so you'll change the Country button to Cowbell. After all, you never know when you'll need more cowbell.

6   Locate the Country button (near the top of the third column). Drag it to the bottom of the first column and release it over the Vocals button.

7   Control-click (or right-click) the Country button. From the shortcut menu choose Instruments > Percussion > Cowbell.

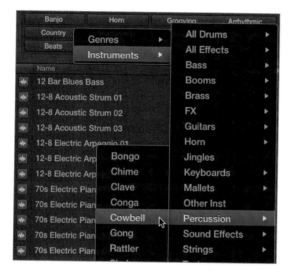

You now have a Cowbell button in your keyword buttons area. Chances are, your new Cowbell button is dimmed. That means there are no cowbell loops in your Loop library. No worries, you'll remedy that in Lesson 7.

NOTE ▶ If you have added other third-party loops or if you had a previous version of GarageBand installed on your computer you may already have a cowbell loop. If so, feel free to click the Cowbell button and listen to your cowbell loops.

8   Click the Reset button.

In the next section you'll put some of your customized buttons to work to find the beats for the song. In Lesson 7, you will create a new cowbell loop and add it to your Loop Library.

Searching with Multiple Keyword Buttons

So far you have searched for loops using text in the search field or a single keyword button at a time. For this exercise you will use three buttons at the same time to narrow the list to find a few perfect beats for the project.

1 In the loop browser, click the Beats button. Notice the number of items in the results list. If you are working with the full set of Apple Loops, your list went from 2,000 to under 500 in one click.

2 Click the Electronic button to further narrow the list of beats.

3 Click the Grooving button. The list narrows by only around 50 loops, so that tells you that most of the Grooving mood beats are also electronic-sounding.

4 Scroll down through the list until you see a family of four loops called Blueprint Beat. Preview each of them, and then add Blueprint Beat 03 and Blueprint Beat 04 to the project.

You have enough loops to start arranging your song, so let's hide the loop browser for now without resetting the keywords. That way if we need to grab another Grooving Beats loop, we don't have to do a new search.

5 Press O, or click the loop browser button to hide it. This will make more room in the tracks area to arrange the regions.

6 Press Command-Right Arrow or use the horizontal zoom slider to adjust the zoom level until the cycle area (bar 1 to bar 20) fills the workspace horizontally.

7   Unmute the Phaser Guitar track and play the project once with all of the parts starting at the same time at the beginning. As expected, all of the parts work together and are in time, though they don't make for a very interesting song—yet.

8   Save your progress.

Now that the basic melody and some rhythm loops are in the timeline, you can move to the next step and start arranging them into a song.

Understanding Melody and Rhythm

What's the difference between melody and rhythm?

Melody is the plot, or story, of a song. It's the memorable part that you hum to yourself when you think of the song, and it's the part other people will remember as well. If you think of the theme song to your favorite movie, you are thinking of the melody. Melody is usually played by the lead instrument, or lead vocal, just as the lead storyline of a movie is played by the lead characters.

In a melody-driven song, you write the melody first, and then add other tracks that work well with the melody. Songs with lyrics usually use the vocals as the melody line.

The song "Dog Walk Ditty," which you worked on in Lesson 2, "Working with Tracks," was melody based. I recorded the guitar melody first, and then added the other instrument parts.

Rhythm is the pulse or heartbeat of the song. Rhythm can be played by one instrument or many different instruments. Rhythm is felt as much as it is heard, and it dictates the pacing of the different instrument parts. Rhythm is usually set by the drums and followed by the other rhythm instruments, such as bass, rhythm guitar, and keyboards. The rhythm of a song may be fast or slow depending on the song's tempo. A slow tempo song might be a ballad with a laid-back rhythm. A fast tempo song might be a rock song with a driving beat.

In a rhythm-driven song, you create the beats, percussion, or rhythm parts first, and then add other instrument parts that fit well with the rhythm. Rhythm-driven songs are often used to score movie trailers (previews), as well as fast-paced promos or commercials. Rap music is often rhythm based, but it depends on the song.

The "Loopy Ringtone" that you are building for this lesson is melody driven. For this piece, I selected the melody loop first. Now that it is in the timeline, the rhythm tracks can be added to supply the heartbeat and driving force that keeps things moving.

With the "Loopy Ringtone," since it is melody driven we can use the changes in the melody to determine how we build the rhythm tracks.

Rhythm tracks can consist of a bass line, a steady rhythm guitar, or drums—whatever the song uses to convey the rhythm. For this song, the pre-recorded drum parts (beats loops) will carry the rhythm.

Arranging Loops in the Timeline

Placing and adding different instrumental parts to build a song is also referred to as *arranging* a song. The basic rhythm loops for this project are already in the timeline.

The trick now is to arrange them in a way that creates an interesting rhythm pattern for the song. Using the same loop or loops over and over might start off sounding cool, but eventually it becomes monotonous. Your goal in the next section is to spread the loops around a bit in the timeline to give each one a chance to be heard and create natural changes in the song's overall rhythm pattern.

Building Rhythm Tracks in the Timeline

In the next series of exercises you'll learn not only how to physically manipulate (arrange) the loops in the timeline but why you'd want to.

Since you are building the song around the melody region (Places Unknown Arpeggio), we'll start there.

> **NOTE** ▶ If you did not complete all of the previous exercises in this lesson, open the project **3-2 Arranging Loops** and save it to your projects folder.

1   Drag the top right edge of the Twilight Piano region toward the right to the beginning of bar 20. Use the yellow cycle area as a guide if needed.

2   Mute all three of the Slow Motion tracks and both Blueprint tracks. You'll unmute and move them as needed.

3   Play the entire piece while listening to the changes in the Twilight Piano melody as it plays.

Here are some things to listen for:

▶   The interesting Doppler-like changes to the music, as if it were on a yo-yo moving closer, then further away repeatedly

▶   Parts of the melody where you anticipate change and it happens just as you thought it would (bars 3, 5, 7)

▶   Part of the melody that repeats (bar 5, 9)

▶   Parts of the melody that build (bar 2, 5, 8)

▶   Parts of the melody that slow, or soften (bars 3, 6)

▶   Any of these musical moments could be excellent places to make dramatic changes in the rhythm track to support the melodic changes.

Let's start with the maracas.

4   Extend the Big Maracas 02 region so that it repeats two times (the loop stops at bar 5).

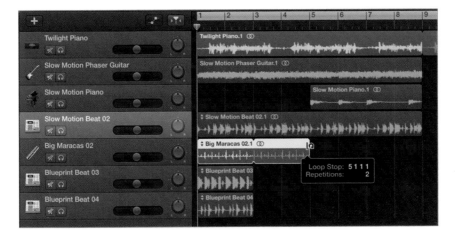

5   Play the beginning of the project to hear the maracas with the melody. So far so good, though I think it's time to kick in the Slow Motion Beat. How about bar 3, where the first part of the melody changes and begins to retreat acoustically as if it is moving away?

6   Unmute the Slow Motion Beat 02 track. Drag the region in that track to the right until it begins at bar 3. This is also where the maracas region repeats. Play the beginning to hear the new arrangement.

Sounds pretty cool. Starts lively, and then the Slow Motion Beat joins in with the maracas and brings the percussion to life as though an audience just joined in with claps and stomps to the beat.

7   Unmute the Blueprint Beat 03 track. Drag the region in that track so that it starts at bar 7. This is where the melody instrumentation change repeats and intensifies as though it is coming toward us. Overlapping the two beats will intensify the beat as well. Also, the new heavier beat indicates this delicate piano melody is ready to switch things up to dance mode.

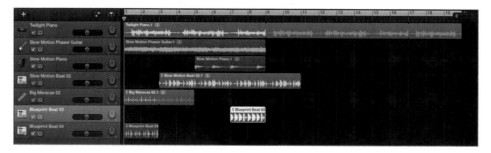

Instead of manually extending the Blueprint Beat 03 region to the end of the project, you'll use a handy looping shortcut.

8   Select the Blueprint Beat 03 region if it isn't already selected. Press L.

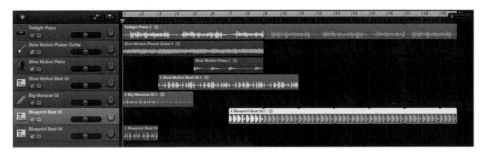

The region extends to the end-of-project marker that is conveniently located for this project at bar 20.

9   Play the project. Sounds good, but the second half gets pretty boring pretty fast with no changes to the rhythm. Let's reuse the Slow Motion Beat 02 region later in the track.

10   Option-drag the Slow Motion Beat 02 region and place the duplicate so it starts at bar 12. Notice that the full name of the duplicate beat is called Slow Motion Beat 02.2 because it is the second version of the original Slow Motion Beat 02 file in the timeline.

NOTE ▶ Remember when you Option-drag to hold the Option key until you release the region; otherwise you'll only move the original region. If this happens, press Command-Z to undo and try again.

Let's trim the beginning of the Slow Motion Beat 02.2 region so that it starts at bar 13. The reason you are trimming rather than dragging it to bar 13 in the first place is because dragging the region so that it stops beyond the end-of-project marker would move the marker accordingly to the end of the last region. Also, I wanted the region to have a different starting beat than the first.

11   Drag the lower-left edge of the Slow Motion Beat 02.2 region right to bar 13.

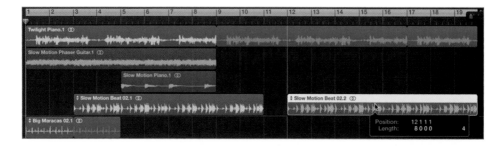

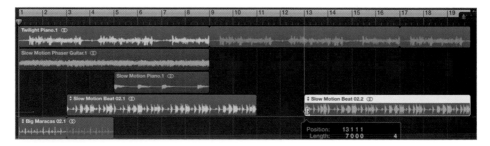

Dragging the lower edge of a region trims the region. Dragging the upper-right edge creates loops (repeated clones) of the original region.

To shorten the length of the Blueprint Beat 03 looped region, let's try a click trick with the Loop tool that only works for trimming repeated segments of a loop.

12 In the Blueprint Beat 03 track, hover over the top half of the repeated segments of the loop. The cursor becomes a Loop tool. Click the loop at bar 17 with the Loop tool.

The repeated segments of the loop stop at bar 17. If you didn't click exactly at bar 17 you can drag the lower-right edge of the region to trim it to bar 17 as needed.

NOTE ▶ Clicking the Loop tool to trim looped segments is a real timesaver compared to manually dragging to trim. But you need to be careful to deselect regions if you don't plan to trim them. Otherwise, it's like running through the track with scissors and accidentally cutting wherever you land.

13 Play the project and save your work.

Well done. You've created a rhythm track that accentuates parts of the melody and punches up the feel of the overall song.

Project Tasks

There are just a few things left to finish the rhythm track. Let's take a few minutes to practice some of your new arrangement skills.

Your goal is to find the Beats loop called Twilight Beat in the loop browser. Drag it to the timeline to create a new track and place it so that it starts at bar 5 and stops at bar 9. Option-drag the Twilight Beat region and place the copy so that it starts at bar 13 and stops at bar 17. Next you'll unmute the bass track and move the region so that it starts at bar 9. Listen to the finished rhythm track. When you're done, you'll reset the keyword buttons and save your progress. Feel free to go ahead, but if you need a little help, use the following steps as a guide.

1   Open the loop browser. Find the loop called Twilight Beat. You may need to click Reset in the loop browser before you search.

2   Drag Twilight Beat from the browser to the tracks area and release it below the lowest track.

3   Clear the search field. Hide the loop browser.

4   In the Twilight Beat track, drag Twilight Beat to the right until starts at bar 5 and stops at bar 9. Option-drag Twilight Beat and release the copy so that it starts at bar 13 and stops at bar 17.

5   Unmute the Slow Motion Phaser Guitar track and move the region down the track until it starts at bar 9. This is the beginning of the second repetition of the melody region. Adding the phaser guitar part at this point in the song supports the melody and the rhythm of the song.

6   Unmute the Blueprint Beat 04 track. Drag the region and place it so that it starts at bar 16. Drag the upper-right edge of the region so that it loops one measure and stops at bar 19.

7   Click the empty space to deselect any selected regions. Play the song to hear the finished rhythm tracks with the melody.

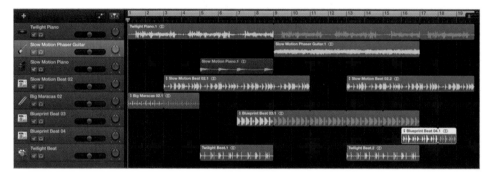

8   When you are finished, display the loop browser and click the Reset button.

9   Save your progress.

This ringtone now has a strong rhythm and will definitely get someone's attention.

Selecting Favorite Loops

The last part of the song to complete is the supporting melody tracks.

With 500 to 2,000 loops to choose from, sometimes it's a good idea to mark your favorites or the loops you plan to use for a specific song. That way, when you're ready to start building the tracks you won't have to break your creative flow to go hunting for loops. Instead, they'll all be located in one category—Favorites.

You can easily locate any loop that is marked as a favorite by using the Favorites button in Button view or the Favorites column in Column view. Since you haven't searched in Column view yet, let's start our search for favorites there.

> **NOTE ▶** If you did not complete all of the previous exercises in this lesson, open the project **3-3 Rhythm Finished** and save it to your projects folder.

1   In the top left of the loop browser, click the Column view button. The loop browser search area changes from Button view to Column view.

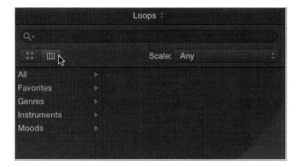

2   Select the Moods category in the first column. A list of all the mood keywords appears in a second column.

3   In the second column, choose Grooving. The third column shows how many Grooving loops are in each keyword instrument or genre category. Scroll through the third column to see the list of descriptive keywords, ranging from Grooving at the top of the column to World at the bottom.

If you aren't sure which keywords to start with, try looking at keywords that describe the melody loop file.

4   In the search field, type *Twilight Piano*. The Descriptive Keyword column shows keywords that apply to that specific loop.

5   In the first column, click Genres. In the second column, the only genre that applies is Urban. That certainly narrows things.

6   In the first column, select Instruments to see a list of instruments used to create the Twilight Piano loop. Since the song doesn't have any bass or synth parts, let's find one of each that will work.

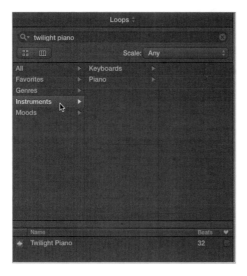

7   Clear the search field. Choose Genres > Urban > Synths. Scroll down through the results list. There are plenty of loops from which to choose; perhaps one of them will work.

8   Click Barricade Arpeggio in the results list. Sounds like it will fit perfectly near the middle of the song. Rather than drag it over, click the checkbox on the Favorites column. The Favorites column is the column of checkboxes at the far right of the results list—the one with a heart in the header.

9   In the search area, select the Favorites category. All of the keywords used by your favorite loop are listed in the second column. And since you have only one favorite marked, it is the only loop in the results list.

Marking favorites is like gathering items in a grocery basket. Let's use the search field to locate the remaining melody loops and mark each as a favorite. When you are finished, all the loops you need to finish the song will be in one place, without crowding the timeline workspace until you need them.

NOTE ▸ Be sure to clear the search field between searches. Also, if in Column view, be sure to click the All category in the first column after you type a name in the search field to begin the search of all loops in the browser.

10 Search for the following loops in the loop browser (using either Column or Button view) and mark each as a favorite:

All Your Base Gated Synth

Rhyming Scheme Sub Bass

Rhyming Scheme Synth Lead

11 Clear the search field if needed. Change the loop browser to Button view if it is in Column view. Click the Favorites button to see all your favorites in the results list.

You have completed your search for the melody loops and marked them as favorites. Now all you have to do is arrange them in the timeline.

Project Tasks

It's time to put all of your skills to work to arrange the rest of the song. Your goal will be to drag each of the favorite loops to the timeline into a new track and then place it where directed. Before you get started, go ahead and change the horizontal zoom in your workspace so that you can see the entire first 20 bars as well as the loop browser. Also drag the top track, Twilight Piano, down to the bottom of the tracks area so you can build the other melody tracks below the main melody track. Drag the muted Slow Motion Piano track below the Twilight Piano track.

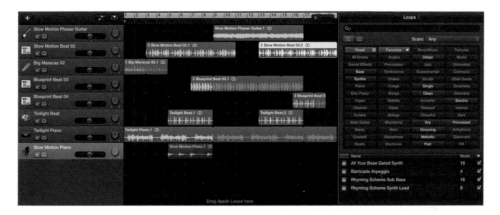

1   Unmute the Solo Motion Piano track. Drag the top-right edge of the region until the loops stop at bar 17.

2   Drag the Barricade Arpeggio loop from the loop browser to the timeline so that it starts at bar 8. Extend it by one measure so that it stops at bar 10. This loop will overlap one measure in either direction of bar 9 when the melody loop repeats. This will act as an acoustic distraction from the melody repetition and an accent to the overall music.

> **TIP ▶** If you know at which measure (bar in the ruler) you want to place a loop, you can use the position overlay and guides to move a loop into position as you initially drag it from the browser. When you release the loop, it is already in the correct position in its own new track.

3   Drag Rhyming Scheme Sub Bass from the browser to the timeline and loop it so that it starts at bar 9 and stops at bar 19.

4   Drag Rhyming Scheme Synth Lead from the browser to the timeline so that it starts at bar 3 and stops at bar 5. Option-drag the Rhyming Scheme Synth Lead region and place the duplicate down the track so that it starts at bar 15 and stops at bar 17.

5   Drag All Your Base Gated Synth from the browser to the timeline so that it starts at bar 13 and stops at bar 17. Hide the loop browser.

6   Play the finished song. Sounds pretty cool, doesn't it?

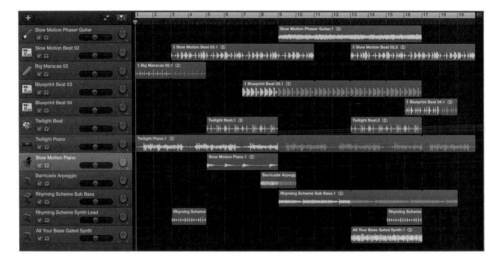

7   In the loop browser, uncheck each of the favorite loops to clear your favorites for the next project. Click the Reset button and hide the loop browser.

> **NOTE ▶** If you did not complete all of the previous exercises in this lesson and you would like to hear the finished project, open the project **3-4 Loopy Ringtone Finished** and save it to your projects folder.

Congratulations! You built a song from scratch using only Apple Loops. Along the way you learned some advanced search techniques, how to customize keyword buttons, and how to arrange loops to build a song.

The song still needs mixing, which you'll learn how to do in Lesson 8, to balance the volume levels between tracks and add effects to enhance the overall sound. The ending also could use a little finessing, which you'll see in Lesson 9, "Sharing Your Finished Projects," when you learn to share the project as a ringtone.

In the next lesson you'll learn how to record and edit Software Instruments.

Bonus Exercise

If you enjoyed arranging the song in this lesson and would like to build another song with Apple Loops, here is a bonus exercise you can complete on your own. This exercise requires the full set of 2,000 loops to complete. If you have only 500 loops, follow along but select different loops to create your own variation of the finished piece.

Instead of a ringtone, you'll create a 30-second song for a company website. They want something sweet, fun, and contemporary but not tacky or overly sappy and sentimental. Sound like fun? (I've been asked to write a piece of music by a client who used these exact words. Says more about the client than the song—but a gig is a gig and the client is always right.)

In step 3 you'll see a list of the loops you need to find and where they go on separate tracks. After the loops have been arranged, you'll change the sound of one instrument.

The finished project is called **3 Sweet Looping Finished**, and you can find it in APTS GarageBand Book Files > Lesson Bonus Projects.

1   Create a new project with the Empty Project template. You'll be prompted to choose the type of track you want to start with; choose "Audio - Record using a microphone or line input."

2   Save the project as *Sweet Looping*.

3   In the loop browser, find the following loops and add them to the timeline accordingly:

   ▶ Sparks Fly Piano: bar 1 to the third beat of bar 9 (9 3 1 1)

   ▶ True Love Electric Piano: bar 1 to bar 15

   ▶ Deep Electric Piano 07: bar 4 to bar 9, Option-drag duplicate to the fourth beat of bar 12 (12 4 1 1). Trim the duplicate region so that it stops at 15 4 1 1.

   ▶ Breathless Piano: bar 13 to 15 2 1 1

   ▶ Cali Vibes Piano: bar 9 to bar 13

   ▶ White Light Sample Vox: bar 8 to 15 3 1 1

   ▶ Super Strength Beat 02: bar 11 to 14 3 1 1

   ▶ Super Strength Beat 01: bar 11 to bar 13

   ▶ Tambourine Tap Topper: bar 9 to bar 12

4   Double-click the Deep Electric Piano 07 track header. Since it is a Software instrument, you can change the instrument. In the Library, choose Synthesizer > Dreamy Bells > Bell.

5   Play the finished song and save your work.

Lesson Review

1.   What is the difference between melody and rhythm?

2.   Do all Apple Loops in the browser have the same tempo and key?

3.   What are the two different ways you can view keywords in the loop browser?

4.   How do you move a keyword button to a new position in the loop browser?

5.   Which side of a loop can be extended in the timeline so it repeats?

6.   Can you change the keyword on a specific button? If so, how?

7.   What happens when you click the Reset button in the loop browser?

8.   How do you reset all of the keyword buttons back to the original names and locations?

Answers

1. Melody is the memorable part of the song; rhythm is the pulse that keeps the tempo.

2. Apple Loops in the browser have a native tempo and key in which they were recorded originally. When you preview them in the browser or add them to a song, they match the tempo and key of the project.

3. You can view keywords in Button or Column view in the loop browser.

4. You can move a keyword button to a new position in the loop browser by dragging it over another button. The two buttons swap positions.

5. You extend or trim a loop from the right side with the Loop tool.

6. You can change the keyword on a specific button. Control-click (or right-click) the button and choose a different keyword from the shortcut menu.

7. When you click the Reset button in the loop browser, all of the buttons become deselected so you can begin a new search.

8. You can reset all of the keyword buttons back to the original names and locations with the Reset control in the Loop preferences.

4

Lesson Files APTS GarageBand Book Files > Lesson 4 > 4-1 Ditty Bass Part 1, 4-2 Bass 1 Recorded, 4-3 Bass Part 2, 4-4 Bass Part 2 Recorded, 4-5 Edit Strings, 4-6 Arrangement Track, 4-7 Finished Ditty

Time This lesson takes approximately 90 minutes to complete.

Goals Record a Software Instrument take

Fix the timing of notes in the Piano Roll Editor

Record multiple takes of a bass part

Choose a take

Edit multiple notes at once in the Piano Roll Editor

Use arrangement markers to copy parts of a song

Recording and Editing Software Instruments

You already have a basic understanding of the GarageBand window, and you have some experience working with tracks. Now it's time to dive in and start filling those tracks with custom music that you create with Software Instruments.

In this lesson, you'll learn recording and editing techniques for building music with Software Instrument regions. You'll also learn how to change instruments for Software Instrument tracks in the timeline.

You have four ways of recording Software Instrument parts into the timeline: single-take recording, multiple-take recording, multiple-track recording, and overdub recording. You'll work with the first three methods in this lesson. Along the way you'll also learn how to edit and fix timing on your Software Instrument recordings. You'll explore the fourth option, overdub recording, in Lesson 7, "Creating Drum and Percussion Tracks," when you use it to record an original hip-hop beat.

Preparing the Project

Let's take a moment to open and save the first project for this lesson before moving on to the main exercises.

1 Open the project **4-1 Ditty Bass Part 1** from the Lesson 4 folder.

2 Save it to your My GarageBand Projects folder on the desktop.

3 Play the project once and listen closely to the bass parts that you will be recording shortly.

This is the same project you worked with in Lesson 2, "Working with Tracks." The difference is that there's a new section at the end that will be used as a bridge between the second verse and second chorus. Those parts have not yet been created. At the end of this lesson you'll use the arrangement track to duplicate parts of the song to build it up to a full song length.

There's just one catch you should be aware of before you get started.

Using Catch Mode to Keep the Playhead Visible

While you record or edit your finished recordings, it's a good idea to be able to see the playhead at all times. When Catch mode is on, the visible section of the tracks area or editor follows the playhead during playback and recording. If Catch mode is turned off, the playhead moves past the right edge of the visible portion of the window because the window doesn't update.

Independent Catch buttons in the tracks area, Audio Editor, and Piano Roll Editor menu bar allow you to turn Catch mode on or off.

Let's look at the project with Catch mode on and off so you understand how it works.

1   Press Command-Right Arrow or drag the horizontal zoom slider in the tracks area to the right to zoom into the timeline until you can see only the intro and the beginning of the verse parts of the song.

2   Check to see if Catch mode is on (the Catch button is blue). If not, click the Catch button to turn on Catch mode.

3   Start playback and watch the playhead. When it gets to around the middle of the tracks area, the playhead remains stationary while the tracks scroll underneath the playhead.

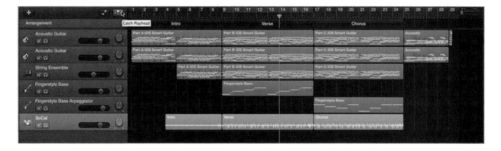

4   Continue playback. Click the Catch button to turn off Catch mode. The playhead continues moving off the right side of the screen.

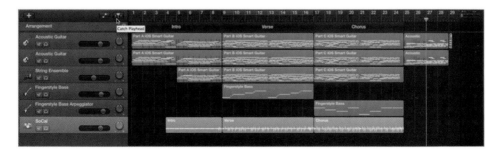

5   Click the Catch button again to "catch" the playhead so that it displays on the screen. The playhead will gradually work its way back to the middle of the tracks area while always staying visible, with the regions scrolling beneath it. When you reach the last measures of the song, the playhead moves toward the right until it reaches the end-of-project marker.

6   Zoom out of the timeline until you can see all the regions in the tracks area again.

Now that you know how Catch mode works, you can make sure it is on when recording in the timeline. That way, you can keep an eye on the recording in real time as it forms a region in the timeline.

Single-Take Recording

A single-take recording begins on a selected track at the playhead position and continues until you stop recording. This is an excellent recording method when you're practicing or just want to quickly record a musical riff, melody, or idea so you don't forget it.

The result is a single region containing whatever notes were played while recording. This method is similar to recording video or using a voice recorder: The hardest part is the performance. Of course, with Software Instrument recordings every part of the recording is editable, so no worries. Also, you'll use keyboard shortcuts whenever possible to keep your hands on your instrument (computer keyboard) rather than a mouse or trackpad.

In the next series of exercises you'll create a single-take recording of the bass part for the Dog Walk Ditty's first verse. Let's get started:

1   Select the Fingerstyle Bass track header. The region within that track is the Fingerstyle Bass part that you will record.

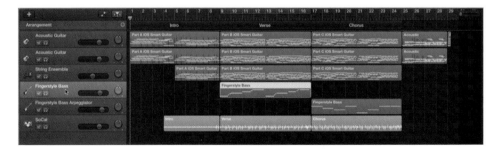

2   Press Command-D to duplicate the selected track. An empty Fingerstyle Bass track appears in the timeline below the original track.

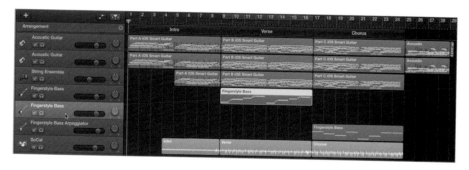

This is the track where you will record your bass part.

3   Press C or click the Cycle button to show the yellow cycle area on the top half of the ruler. The cycle area should be from bar 9 to bar 17.

NOTE ▶ If for some reason you do not already have a cycle area between bars 9 and 17, drag the cycle area to create one.

4   Press the Up Arrow key to select the first Fingerstyle Bass track. Press S to solo the selected track. Press E to show the selected region in the Score Editor.

5   Press the Spacebar to start playback and listen to the bass part. Follow along with the playhead in the editor as it plays the notes in the Fingerstyle Bass region.

The part is very simple to play (by design). Let's give it a try using your computer keyboard.

Playing Music with Your Computer Keyboard

You can play and record Software Instruments using an external MIDI music keyboard, the onscreen keyboard, or musical typing. In the exercises for this lesson, you'll use musical typing to turn your Mac computer's keyboard into a fully functional MIDI keyboard.

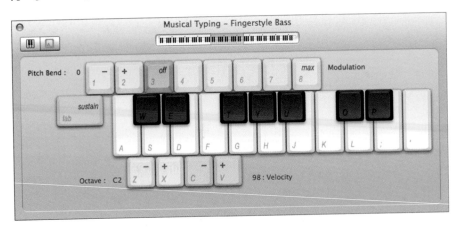

The Musical Typing keyboard shows which musical keys correspond with the keys on your computer keyboard. Notice that the Tab key works as a sustain pedal. The Z and X keys will modulate the octave lower and higher, respectively, while C and V lower and raise the velocity (the relative volume is based on how hard you strike the key). You can click the keys on the Musical Typing window with your cursor or play them on your computer keyboard.

1   Choose Window > Show Musical Typing or press Command-K. The Musical Typing window appears over your workspace. Luckily, it is a floating window so you can move it anywhere you'd like on your screen.

NOTE ► You can click the notes in the Score Editor to see the name (key) of each note and octave. C2 is Middle C on the keyboard. C3 is one octave higher, C1 is one octave lower, and so on. The blue area on the mini keyboard at the top of the Musical Typing window shows which octave is active in the window.

2   Drag the Musical Typing window below the Fingerstyle Bass track header so that you
can still see the Fingerstyle Bass region in the track and the notes in the Score Editor.

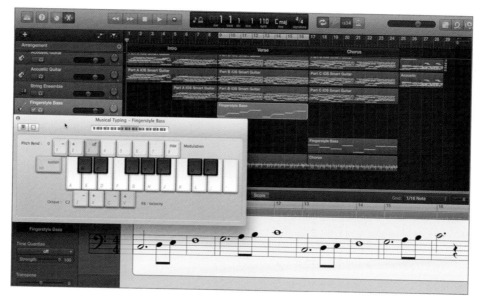

3   Start playback. The notes on the Musical Typing keyboard darken as they are played.
Watch carefully to see the pattern of the notes that are played.

The good news is that I intentionally composed this part so it would be easy to play
and remember. All you have to do is play the middle keys on your computer keyboard
sequentially: A, S, D, F, G, H, J, K, L. They correspond with the musical notes (the first
eight white piano keys) shown on the Musical Typing keyboard: C, D, E, F, G, A, B, C.

4   Stop playback. Press each of the keys on your keyboard in order: A, S, D, F, G, H, J, K, L.
Now that you've played the notes, you can practice the timing.

5   Click the Metronome button in the toolbar to turn on the click track.

NOTE ▶ The shortcut K to turn on or off the metronome won't work when the
Musical Typing window is displayed because K is one of the keyboard keys used to
play music. The same applies to any keyboard shortcuts that consist of a letter without
a modifier key.

6   Start playback and practice along with the prerecorded bass part. You can use the
audio of the Fingerstyle Bass track and the visual of the playhead moving over notes
in the Score Editor as guides. Unsolo the Fingerstyle Bass track and practice a few
times with the full song. When you are ready to record, stop playback.

It's time to lay down a track. That's musician-speak for recording an instrument onto a track.

Recording a Single Take in the Timeline

You have all the skills to record this part. All you need to do is hide the editor, turn off
Cycle mode, and set your count-in. Cycle mode is used for multitake and overdub recording. Although using the cycle area was useful for practicing your part, it must be turned
off to perform a single-take recording. Remember, many keyboard shortcuts do not work
while the Musical Typing window is open, so you'll need to manually click the buttons to
turn off Cycle mode and hide the editor.

1   Click the Cycle button to turn it off.

2   Click the Editors button to hide the editor.

3   Drag the Musical Typing window to the bottom of the tracks area.

The last thing to do before recording is set a "count-in" so that the metronome will click for one full bar (four clicks in this case) or two full bars (eight clicks) before the actual recording begins. The count-in gives you a "one-two-three-go" so that you don't have to start playing the instant you click Record. The Count-In button is on the left side of the Metronome button and turns purple when it is turned on.

4   Click the Count-In button to turn it on and set the count-in to two bars so you will hear eight clicks before you start recording.

5   Choose Record > Count-In > 2 Bars.

6   Make sure the empty Fingerstyle Bass track is selected.

7   Click bar 9 on the ruler to move the playhead to that position.

In GarageBand, the color red is only used for recording. During a recording, the record button turns red, whereas a red region appears in the timeline as you record to represent the live recording. Also, the playhead turns red during recording, as does the LCD display during recording count-in.

Starting the instant you click Record, the playhead will move back two measures from its current position. You will hear the count-in for eight beats as the playhead moves across the two bars in the ruler toward the record-start position. Time to record—good luck!

8   Click the Record button in the transport controls on the toolbar. Record the bass part that you practiced. A red region appears in the selected track as you record. The region doesn't appear until you record the first note. When you are finished recording, press the Spacebar to stop recording.

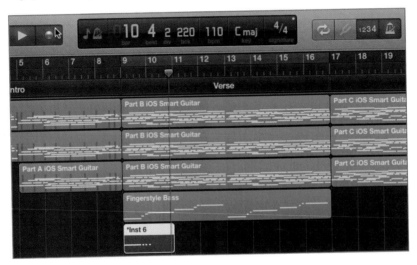

Notice that the newly recorded region changes from red to green, indicating it is a Software Instrument region.

9   If you don't like your recording and want to try again, press Command-Z or choose Edit > Undo Recording. Repeat step 8.

10 Press Command-S to save your finished recording. Close the Musical Typing window.

NOTE ► Saving is an important part of recording because it saves the recording with the project file. You still have the option to delete or edit the region at another time.

The recorded region is named after the track and should look a lot like the original Fingerstyle Bass region in the track above it.

11 Mute the original Fingerstyle Bass track. Listen to your recording with the rest of the tracks. How does it sound?

Don't worry if it isn't perfect; you'll fix the timing in the Piano Roll Editor next.

Fixing Notes in the Piano Roll Editor

Previously, you used the Score Editor as a guide while you practiced the bass part. For this exercise you'll work with the Piano Roll Editor to modify the length and position of the individual bass notes to fix any timing issues your recording may have.

> **NOTE ▶** If you did not complete all of the previous exercises in this lesson, open the project **4-2 Bass 1 Recorded** and save it to your projects folder. In this version of the exercise, you'll work with a bass part that I recorded.

1 Move the playhead to bar 9 in the timeline.

2 Select the Fingerstyle Bass track containing your new recording.

3 Press E to display the Score Editor. Click the Piano Roll button to display the Piano Roll Editor.

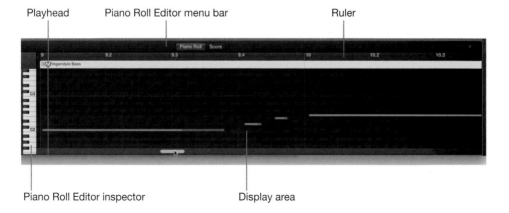

Playhead   Piano Roll Editor menu bar   Ruler

Piano Roll Editor inspector   Display area

4   Swipe over the region in the Piano Roll Editor display area left or right, or drag the horizontal slider at the bottom of the editor (which appears when you swipe) to position the beginning of the region (bar 9) at the beginning of the visible area of the editor. Also adjust the horizontal zoom slider in the editor or pinch on your touchpad as needed until the grid shows each beat in the measure. The beats are listed in the editor ruler as a decimal point after the bar number, such as 9.3 for the third beat of bar 9.

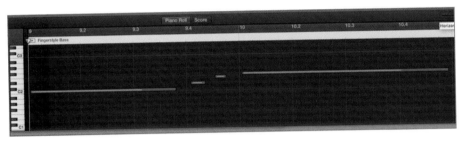

Human performances usually aren't perfect. Sometimes the imperfections in music add subtle nuances and feeling to a song. In fact, you probably could get away with your recording as is, with no additional editing. However, since you need to learn how to edit anyway, let's fix it.

Each note (represented by a green bar in the Piano Roll Editor) should start exactly on a beat. The long notes should start exactly at the beginning of a measure (bar). To fix the timing or position of a note in the Piano Roll Editor, you simply click and drag the note in the middle to move it, and on the edge to trim or lengthen it.

5   Drag the first note in the region to the left until it starts at the first beat (beginning) of bar 9. Chances are, your first note will not look exactly like the one shown in the screen-shot. Regardless of its length, you'll need to move the first note to the beginning of bar 9.

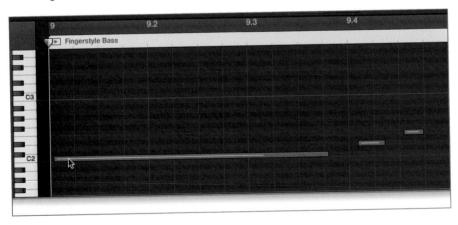

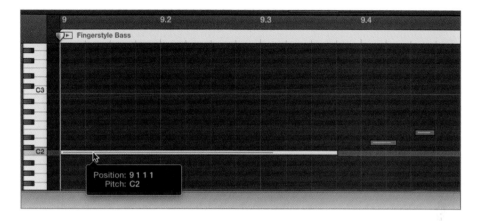

Notice that when you select a note, the Notes tab at the top of the Piano Roll Editor inspector turns blue.

6   Drag the second note to the fourth beat of bar 9 (9.4).

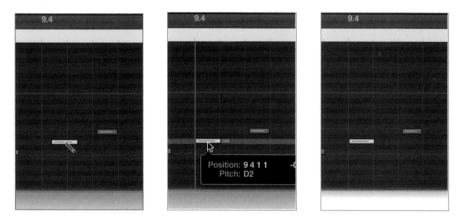

NOTE ▶ If your second and third notes are significantly shorter or longer than a quarter of a beat, you can trim the edges so that they fit between the gridlines, like the notes pictured in the screenshots.

As you can see, fixing notes individually is not difficult. However, if you are working with a long region or a lot of notes, this process can become rather tedious.

Quantizing Notes in a Region

Rather than manually moving each and every note in a region to fix the timing, you can *quantize* the timing. Quantizing is a digital music term for automatically fixing timing based on set parameters. In this case, GarageBand will automatically move all the notes to the nearest gridline based on the settings in the Piano Roll Editor inspector.

You can use the Time Quantize button to fix the timing of all the notes in an entire region or selected notes. These timing changes are nondestructive. The original timing is never lost, so you can turn off Time Quantize at any time to return to the original recorded timing.

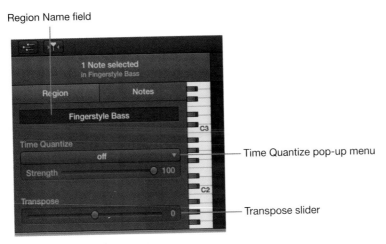

Region Name field

Time Quantize pop-up menu

Transpose slider

One thing to keep in mind is that the Time Quantize feature is selection based. If you have a note selected, only that note will be fixed. To fix all the notes in a region at once, you need to first deselect any notes. The Piano Roll Editor inspector controls change depending on whether you have a region (all notes) or individual notes selected. The Region or Notes tabs change automatically based on your selections.

1   Click any empty space in the editor display area to deselect all notes within the region. The top of the inspector shows which items will be modified.

2   In the Piano Roll Editor inspector, type *My* in the Region Name field so that the name of the region changes to *My Fingerstyle Bass.* Press Return to implement the change. This will help distinguish your recording from the one provided in the starting version of the project.

NOTE ▶ The top of the Piano Roll Editor inspector shows what is currently selected, and therefore what will be modified by changes to the controls. If your inspector shows no regions selected, go up to the timeline and select the My Fingerstyle Bass region.

3   In the Piano Roll Editor inspector, click the Time Quantize pop-up menu and choose 1/16 Note. Perfect timing—instantly!

The Strength slider is only available when an entire region is selected. Leave the Strength slider set to 100. Lowering the strength decreases the amount of quantization.

4   Press E to hide the Piano Roll Editor. Press K to kill the click track (to turn off the metronome).

5   Play the project from bar 9 to 17 to hear your edited recording in action. Well done!

Now that your recording is finished, you don't need the original Fingerstyle Bass track. To delete the track, let's use the shortcut menu in the track's header.

6   Control-click (or right-click) the track header for the top Fingerstyle Bass track. Choose Delete Track from the shortcut menu. Click OK in the warning dialog that says "There are regions in this track!"

7   Save your progress.

Project Tasks

You've successfully recorded a single-take Software Instrument Bass part. In a few minutes you'll work with the Smart Controls and the arpeggiator to record a more complex bass part using multiple-take recording. For now, you'll hone your current skills to learn and practice the new bass part.

Create a cycle area from bar 17 to 25. Display the Note Pad to see which notes you need to play for the Bass Part 2 Chorus. Open the Musical Typing window and play the new part along with the song. Use the Score Editor to look at the notes you need to play. Remember that you are just learning the individual notes. You'll add the arpeggiator in the next section.

The keys you will be playing on your computer keyboard/Musical Typing window are K, G, F, K, A, F, K. Once you have practiced the part, stop playback.

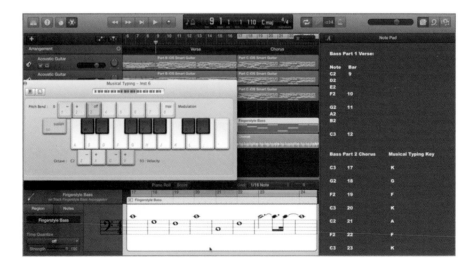

Working with Smart Controls and the Arpeggiator

For the second bass recording, you'll work with the arpeggiator to create a bass part that accompanies itself. The arpeggiator plays a sequence of notes for every note you press. If you play a chord, each note of the chord is played a note at a time in the specified pattern or preset. The best way to get a feel for the arpeggiator is to explore the settings already applied to the region in the Fingerstyle Bass Arpeggiator track. Keep in mind that the arpeggiator is applied to an entire track, not the specific region, so any region that you add or any playing you record to an arpeggiated track will play the arpeggiated pattern unless you turn it off.

1   Close the Musical Typing window to make more room in your workspace.

2   Select the Fingerstyle Bass Arpeggiator track header, if it is not already selected.

3   In the toolbar at the top of the window, click the Smart Controls button.

The Smart Controls pane replaces the editor at the bottom of the window.

The controls that look like they are mounted on a bass guitar can be used to adjust the sound of the instrument, but you can ignore them for now. For this exercise you'll focus on the Arpeggiator button and Arpeggiator pop-up menu located in the upper right of the Smart Controls pane.

4   Solo the Fingerstyle Bass Arpeggiator track. Start playback. What you hear is the sound of the Groovy Cycle 01 Arpeggiator preset.

5   Continue playback. Click the Arpeggiator button to turn it off. The notes play one at a time, just as you practiced them in the project tasks.

6   Click the Arpeggiator button to turn it back on. Stop playback.

7   Click the Arpeggiator pop-up menu to see the various options.

▶   Note Order is the direction of arpeggiated notes.

▶   Rate is the note value for arpeggiated notes based on the song tempo.

▶   Octave Range is how many octaves the arpeggio covers.

▶   Arpeggiator Presets are listed below the line starting with Classic Cycle 01.

8   Start playback. Try several arpeggio presets. They all sound pretty good. When you are finished trying presets, choose the Groovy Cycle 01 preset. Stop playback.

Now that you know how to turn on the arpeggiator and change the preset, you're ready to record.

Preparing the Project

You still need to create a track to record your second bass part for the chorus section of the song. Let's go ahead and rename the track. Also, it wouldn't hurt to practice one more time before recording.

1   Select the Fingerstyle Bass Arpeggiator track if it is not already selected.

2   Press Command-D to duplicate the track.

3   Control-click (or right-click) the new track's header and choose Rename Track from the shortcut menu. Type *My Arpeggiator Bass* in the track's name field. Press Return to set the new name.

4   Look at the Smart Controls pane for the new track. Notice that the Arpeggiator settings are already on and ready to go. That's because duplicating a track also duplicates the track's instrument and settings. Did you notice that the new track was soloed because the track you duplicated had the Solo button on at the time you created the duplicate track?

5   Press B to hide the Smart Controls pane. Press Command-K to open the Musical Typing window.

6   Move the Musical Typing window to the empty space at the bottom of the tracks area where the editors and Smart Controls would be if they were showing.

7   Start playback and practice the part a few more times using the Note Pad as a reminder of which notes (keys) to play (type) on the Musical Typing keyboard.

TIP ▶ If practicing or recording with an arpeggiated Software Instrument is distracting you from concentrating on your performance timing, you can always turn off the arpeggiator in the Smart Controls and then turn it back on after you record.

8   Save your progress.

It's time to try recording multiple takes of the arpeggiator bass part. The good news is that with multiple takes, you can pick which take you want to use and still edit it to fix any performance issues you may have while recording.

Recording Multiple Takes

Multiple-take recording means you can record multiple versions (takes) in succession. Once you stop recording, you can preview the various takes and choose which one you want to use in the project.

The secret to multiple-take recording involves the Cycle Recording preference and the cycle area in the timeline. During multiple-take recording, a new take is recorded each time the cycle repeats. Let's try it.

NOTE ▶ If you did not complete all of the previous exercises in this lesson, open the project **4-3 Bass Part 2** and save it to your projects folder. Also, you'll need to Press Command-K to show the Musical Typing window before continuing on with the next step.

1   Choose GarageBand > Preferences.

2   In General Preferences, make sure Cycle Recording is deselected.

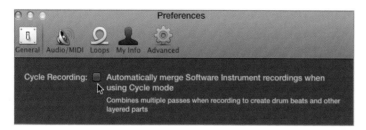

If Cycle Recording is selected, each recording cycle is combined within one take. You'll try this in Lesson 7, "Creating Drum and Percussion Tracks," to create a complex drum beat. With Cycle Recording deselected, you will record a new take with each cycle.

3   Close the General Preferences.

4   Turn on the metronome.

5   Select the My Arpeggiator Bass track if it is not already selected. Recordings always go to the selected track.

Your goal is to record at least four full takes before you stop recording. Four takes will give you plenty to choose from when you need to select the best take.

6   Click the Record button to begin multiple-take recording. You will hear the count-in before recording starts. Play the bass part on your computer's keyboard. After at least three full cycles, stop recording. You are welcome to record more takes if you wish. With each cycle you will see a red region for the live recording, whereas a green region remains underneath for the previous finished take.

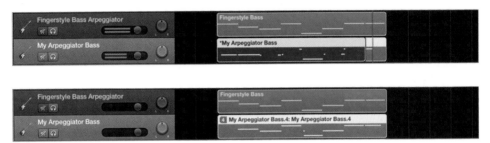

Take a look at the finished multiple-take region. The number in the upper-left corner of the region shows the current take number. The name of the region is the same as the name of the track, with the addition of a decimal point and take number at the end. In this case, it reads My Arpeggiator Bass.4.

7   Turn off the metronome. Close the Musical Typing window and hide the Note Pad.

8   Save your project.

You've finished recording multiple takes of the second bass part. In the next section you'll choose a take to use in the finished project.

Choosing a Take

After you've recorded a multiple-take region, you can use the Takes pop-up menu in the upper-left corner of the region to change to a different take. In this exercise you'll evaluate the different takes and choose the one closest to the original Fingerstyle Bass part that you used as a guide. Later, you can fix the timing of the performance in the Piano Roll Editor.

> **NOTE** ▶ If you did not record a multiple-take region in the previous exercise, open the project **4-4 Bass Part 2 Recorded** and save it to your projects folder.

1   Select the multiple-take region in your timeline and press Command-Right Arrow or the horizontal zoom slider to zoom into the region until it is easy to compare the notes (dashes) in the multiple-take region with the Fingerstyle Bass guide region.

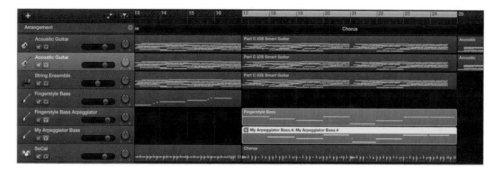

2   In the upper-left corner of the multiple-take region, click the number (4 in the screenshot) to open the Takes pop-up menu. The Takes menu lists each take, along with an option to delete unused takes or delete the current take. From the Takes menu, choose Take 1.

3   Listen to Take 1 with the other bass part. Then unsolo both arpeggiator bass tracks, and mute the original Fingerstyle Base Arpeggiator track. Listen to your bass part with the rest of the tracks.

4   Choose each take and listen to it with the song. If needed, solo your take with the original arpeggiator bass track to hear them together. When you have determined which take is best, keep it selected and move on to the next step.

    NOTE ▶ If you are working with the prebuilt project **4-4 Bass Part 2 Recorded, Take 1** is the best take.

5   Double-click the multiple-take region with the best take showing to open it in the
Piano Roll Editor.

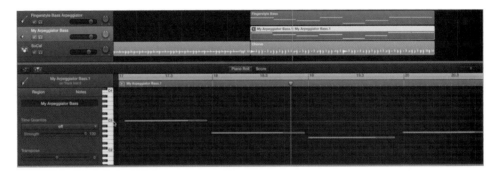

NOTE ▶ If the Score Editor opens, click the Piano Roll button to switch editors. If you
don't see the selected region in the Piano Roll Editor, click the Catch button in the
upper-left corner of the editor and start playback. If you don't see any dashes (MIDI
notes) on the grid, you may be looking at the wrong octave range within the region in
the editor. Swipe up or down until you see the C3–C2 octave range in the visible area.
Use the vertical keyboard at the left of the editor as a guide.

Look at the notes in the Piano Roll Editor to see where they begin. Chances are, the
notes do not begin precisely at the beginning of bars or beats as they should.

6   Adjust the horizontal zoom slider in the editor until you see each beat in the ruler,
four beats (indicated with decimal points) per measure.

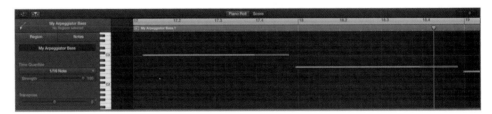

Each note starts at the beginning of a measure (bar), so you can quantize the notes to
the nearest 1/4 note (beat).

7   Select the first note, and choose "1/4 note" from the Time Quantize pop-up menu.

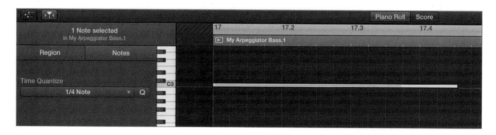

The selected note moves to the beginning of the 17th measure (bar 17).

8   Press Command-A, or choose Edit > Select All to select all the notes in the region. The top of the Piano Roll Editor inspector shows that eight notes have been selected. Click the Q (Quantize button) to apply 1/4 note quantizing to all of the selected notes.

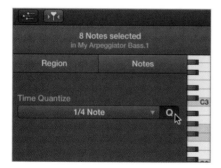

All of the selected notes move into position so they start precisely at the beginning of each measure.

9   Zoom out of the Piano Roll Editor until you can see all the notes in the region to inspect their quantized positions.

Perfect!

10   Press E to hide the editor.

11   Delete the Fingerstyle Bass Arpeggiator track. Click OK in the warning dialog.

12   Turn off Cycle mode.

13   Adjust the zoom level in the tracks area until you can see all the regions.

14   Save your project.

All the bass parts have been recorded and the workspace is displaying only the tracks area and headers. It's time to finish this song.

Editing Multiple Notes Simultaneously in the Editor

To complete this song, your next task is to clean up the busy strings regions. If you recall, the regions in the String Ensemble track are duplicates of the iOS Smart Guitar regions. The busy guitar fingering works fine for the guitar, but it is too much for strings in this song. In this exercise, you'll open the first strings region in the Piano Roll Editor, and then select and delete all of the notes in the middle of the grid. That way, all you are leaving are the highest and lowest notes. Let's give it a try.

NOTE ▶ If you did not complete all of the previous exercises in this lesson, open the project **4-5 Edit Strings** and save it to your projects folder.

1 Select the String Ensemble track header. Press E to open the selected track in the Piano Roll Editor.

2 Adjust the horizontal zoom in the editor until the first region (Part A iOS Smart Guitar) fills most of the visible area.

3 Drag the top edge of the Piano Roll Editor upward to expand the editor and give you more room to work.

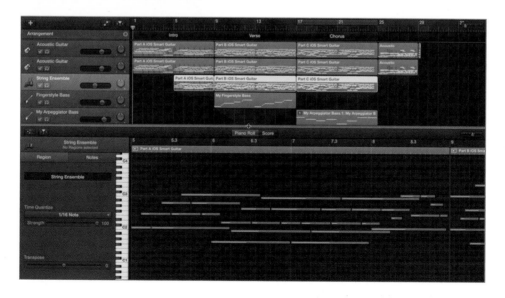

Remember, your goal is to delete middle notes; you'll keep the highest and lowest notes.

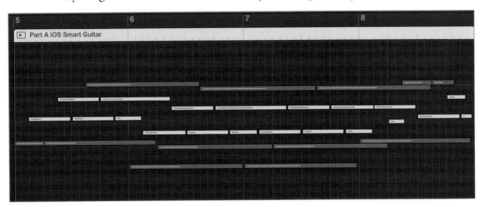

Delete the selected notes shown here

4   In the Part A region in the editor, click the empty grid above the first played note at the beginning of bar 5. Be careful not to click the edge of the region in the editor or you will trim the beginning of the region.

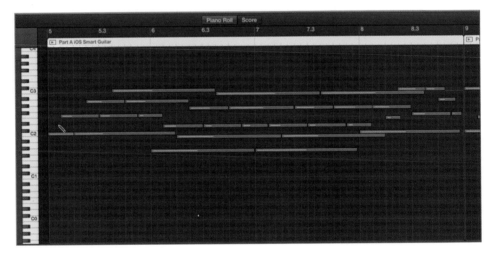

5   Drag up and to the right across the middle notes as shown to select them all at once.

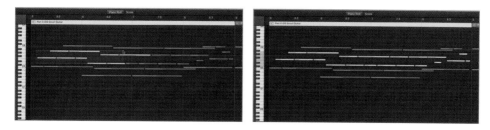

6   Press Delete. The notes are removed from the region.

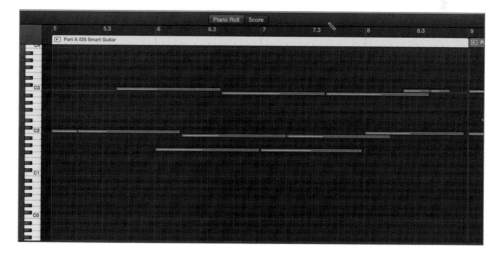

NOTE ▸ You can also click to select individual notes, or drag across a smaller group of notes to delete them in smaller sections if it is easier. The end result will sound the same.

7   Play the first part of the song to hear the edited strings region.

8   Save your progress.

Wow. The strings part sounds so much better. Instead of competing with the guitar part, it now feels like a supporting track.

Project Tasks

Now that you know how to clean up extraneous notes in the Piano Roll Editor, you can work on the Part B and Part C regions in the String Ensemble track. Use your best judgment when selecting "middle" notes and deleting them. The good news is that every note works, so if you delete too many or too few it will still sound great. Remember, you are just making it sound less busy. Play the song to hear the edited string regions with the rest of the song.

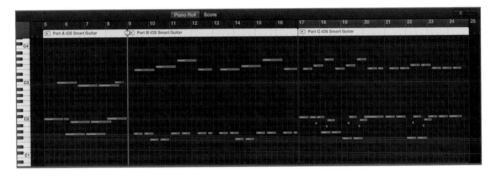

Edited regions with fewer notes.

When you are finished, drag the top edge of the Piano Roll Editor down to the lower third of the window. Don't forget to save your work and close the editor.

Copying Parts of a Song with the Arrangement Track

In Lesson 1, "Working with a GarageBand Project," you worked with arrangement markers in the arrangement track to rename the different sections of this song. Arrangement markers can also be used to move, copy, or delete parts of a song such as the chorus or verse. In this exercise you'll create a new arrangement marker for the bridge section at the end of the song. Then you'll copy and move the verse and chorus parts to lengthen the song. Finally, you'll add an outro (end) to the song. All of this can be done with arrangement markers.

> NOTE ▶ If you did not complete all of the previous exercises in this lesson, open the project **4-6 Arrangement Track** and save it to your projects folder.

1   Click the Add button (+) in the arrangement track header to create a new arrange-
    ment marker. The new arrangement marker appears after the last arrangement
    marker currently in the track (Chorus).

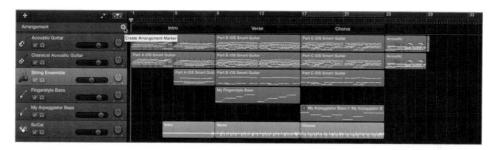

The new marker is already called Bridge, so you won't need to rename it. The marker
is, however, a bit too long for this piece, so let's trim it to fit the part. First, you'll need
to move the little region at the end that isn't actually part of the bridge.

2   Zoom into the bridge section of the timeline. The short region at the end is the last
    chord of the song. Drag the short region toward the right and place it at bar 36 to get
    it out of the way.

3   Drag the right edge of the Bridge arrangement marker to bar 29.

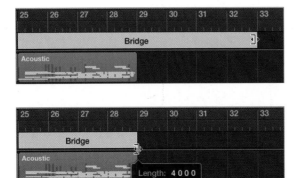

The bridge section of the song is now the same length as the bridge part.

It's time to start copying parts to build the full song. This song will have a total of seven parts: Intro, Verse, Chorus, Verse, Bridge, Chorus, and Outro.

4   Zoom out of the timeline as needed until you see the end-of-project marker at bar 46.

5   Option-drag the empty space on the Verse arrangement marker to the right and place the duplicate after the chorus at bar 25. Release the marker before you release the Option key.

Amazing. The arrangement marker and all of the regions within that section of the song are copied simultaneously.

6 Option-drag the Chorus arrangement marker to bar 37 so the copy starts after the bridge section.

Notice that the little part of the song that you moved out of the way continues to stay the same distance from the end of the song. It just keeps getting moved toward the right with each duplicate section.

The last section to Option-drag is the Intro, which will be repurposed as the Outro with a few minor modifications.

7 Option-drag the Intro arrangement marker to the end of the song and place the duplicate at bar 45.

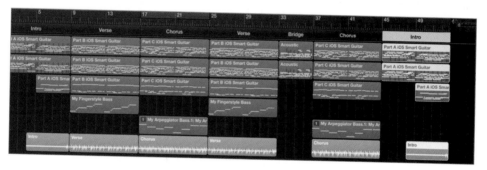

8 Click the name Intro on the last arrangement marker and choose Outro from the pop-up menu.

9 In the Outro section of the song, drag the left edge of the region in the String Ensemble track to extend it to the beginning of the section (bar 45).

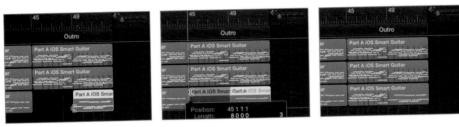

10 Extend the Verse drummer region in the second verse section to bar 37 so that the bridge will share the drummer region.

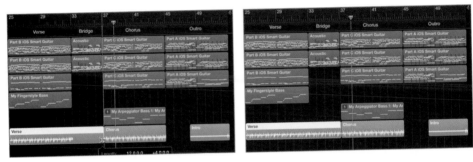

11 Move the drummer region in the Outro so that it starts at bar 45 and ends at 50.

12 Zoom in as needed to drag the short region (past the end-of-project marker) to the left and place it at the end of the Outro section in the Acoustic Guitar track (bar 53).

NOTE ▶ This final chord for the end of the song was not recorded. Rather, it was created in the Piano Roll Editor.

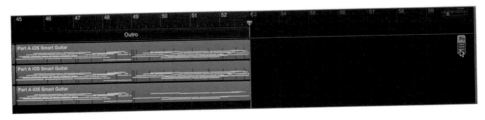

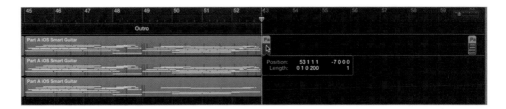

The end-of-project marker automatically moves one bar to the right of the last region in the song—in this case, bar 54.

13 Zoom out of the timeline until you can see the entire song. Play it once to hear how all of the parts work together. Save your project.

> **NOTE ▶** If you did not complete all of the previous exercises in this lesson and want to see the finished song, open the project **4-7 Finished Ditty** and save it to your projects folder.

Congratulations. You recorded and edited two different Software Instrument bass guitar parts. Along the way you also trimmed excess notes from the strings parts and used the arrangement track to build the finished song.

Project Tasks

You may have noticed that the bridge section is missing strings and bass regions. Though traditionally the bridge of a song indicates a change, this one feels a little lacking. If you'd like to finish building the bridge section, feel free. Consider duplicating the guitar part to the strings and/or bass tracks. Then remove notes to clean it up. You could also try recording a new part using either single-take or multiple-take recording. Have fun. When you are finished, save your project.

Recording Multiple Tracks

The last recording feature you'll explore in this lesson is recording to multiple tracks. For this feature, you'll open the Keyboard project template. This is more of an experimental section to show you how to record to multiple tracks. One of the most common uses for multiple track recording is when you want to record a microphone with an instrument. In this example you'll record a voice track with the built-in microphone while simultaneously playing and recording a software instrument track with the Musical Typing window. If you have a MIDI keyboard connected to the computer you can record with that device instead of Musical Typing.

You need an audio interface connected to the computer to record multiple audio instruments such as two guitars simultaneously. To record multiple software instrument tracks you will need to use an external audio interface or use the Audio MIDI Setup utility on your Mac to create an aggregate device.

> **MORE INFO** ▸ You can learn more about the Audio MIDI Setup utility by quitting GarageBand and opening the utility. Go to Go > Utilities > Audio MIDI Setup. Once the utility opens, go to the Help menu and read how it works.

What notes you play, and which Software Instruments you choose to record, will be up to you.

1   Choose File > New. Click the New Project button in the Project Chooser and choose the Keyboard Collection template. Click Choose.

The Keyboard Collection template opens.

2   Save the project as *Multi-track Recording Test* to your projects folder.

The project has the Smart Controls pane showing, along with many prebuilt empty keyboard tracks.

3   Press B to hide the Smart Controls pane.

4   Press Command-K to open the Musical Typing window.

5   Select the first track, and then play a few keys on the Musical Typing keyboard.

6   Press the Down Arrow key to select a track to hear how it sounds; repeat to audition additional tracks.

This project template is preloaded with a lot of different Software Instrument keyboard tracks so you can sample and compare them.

7   Select the track with the keyboard sound that you want to record. Click the Add Track button.

8   In the New Track dialog choose the Microphone icon to create an audio track using a microphone. In the Details pane at the bottom of the New Track dialog, leave the default Input setting (Input 1). Select the checkbox "I want to hear my instrument as I play and record" if it is not already selected. Don't worry about the other settings at

this time. Click Create. You may see an Avoid feedback warning dialog that says you need to use headphones to avoid feedback. If so, click OK on the warning dialog.

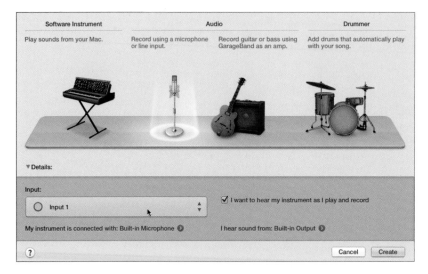

Next you need to set the input to your computer's built-in microphone. The easiest way to do that is through the GarageBand Preferences.

9   Choose GarageBand > Preferences. In the Audio/MIDI preferences pane, select Built-in Microphone from the Input Device pop-up menu. Your other Audio/MIDI preferences may differ from the screen shot depending on your system settings and equipment. Close Preferences.

NOTE ▶ You can also set the Input for an audio track in the Smart Controls inspector.

The new audio track you created should be in the timeline directly below the track you selected to record your musical typing.

You already know that if you want to record to a single track you simply select the track and record. To record to multiple tracks, you need to arm them with Record Enable buttons.

10 Choose Track > Track Header > Show Record Enable Button.

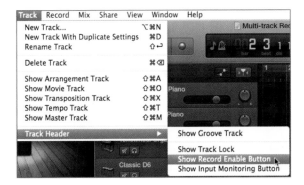

Record Enable buttons appear on each track. The Record Enable button on the selected track is red to indicate the selected track is targeted for recording. However, since you are recording to two different tracks, and only one track can be selected at a time, you'll have to arm the tracks. How? Just click the Record Enable button. When it turns red with a white center, it is armed to record even if the track isn't selected. The Audio 1 Record Enable button will flash, while the Software Instrument track's button remains solid red. Clicking the Record Enable buttons again will turn them off.

11 Click the Record Enable button on the audio track you just created, and the track you want to use for recording musical typing so that both are armed (red).

It's also a good idea to monitor the input of your audio track so you can hear your microphone through headphones along with the musical typing.

NOTE ▶ If you do not see the Input Monitoring button, Control-click (or right-click) the Audio 1 track header and choose Track Header Components > Show input Monitoring from the shortcut menu.

12 Click the Record button in the transport controls and play a few notes on the Musical Typing keyboard. At the same time, speak, sing, or whistle toward the built-in microphone.

13 When you are finished, stop recording.

The number of tracks you can record simultaneously is only limited by your audio input device.

Experiment with the different sounds. If you have a MIDI keyboard attached that is also an audio interface, you may be able to record more tracks simultaneously. In Lesson 5, "Recording and Editing Audio Tracks," you'll explore recording vocal tracks. In Lesson 6, "Working with Electric Guitars," you'll explore guitar recording.

Lesson Review

1. What button determines if the playhead stays in the visible area of the window or continues off the right edge of the window?

2. What window allows you to use your computer's keyboard as a MIDI instrument?

3. Where is the control that lets you make multiple-take recordings of a Software Instrument rather than a merged recording?

4. Is Cycle mode required for single-take recording?

5. How do you choose between takes in multiple-take recording?

6. If you quantize a region in the Piano Roll Editor, what will happen?

7. What happens if you Option-drag an arrangement marker?

8. Which controls need to be turned on in the track header to record to multiple tracks?

Answers

1. The Catch button, if turned on, keeps the playhead in the visible area of the window. When it is turned on, the window is in Catch mode.

2. The Musical Typing window allows you to use your computer's keyboard as a MIDI instrument

3. In GarageBand General Preferences, you will find a control that you deselect for multiple takes or select for merged Software Instrument recordings.

4. Cycle mode must be turned off to record a single take.

5. You can click the Takes menu in the upper-left corner of a multiple-take region to change takes.

6. Quantizing a region in the Piano Roll Editor will fix the timing of all the MIDI note events according to the specified value, such as 1/16 or 1/4 notes, which correspond to lines in the Piano Roll Editor grid.

7. If you Option-drag an arrangement marker, all the regions within that marker will be copied, along with the marker, and moved to wherever you drag the marker. This technique is useful for duplicating parts of the song such as the verse and chorus.

8. The Record Enable buttons need to be turned on in each track that you want to arm for recording.

5

Lesson 5

Recording and Editing Audio Tracks

When you record live audio into GarageBand, the recordings appear as audio regions in audio tracks. The setup for recording audio tracks is the same regardless of the instrument. The exception is if you are recording electric guitar or bass, which use a different type of audio track. You'll learn all about electric guitar and bass tracks in Lesson 6, "Working with Electric Guitars."

The audio instrument you will be working with for this lesson is the human voice—in other words, vocals. Vocal audio tracks can be either musical parts performed by a vocalist (singer) or spoken words such as voice-over or narration. Since all of the other lessons in this book deal with musical tracks, I'm going to change things a bit and have you work with a nonmusical project. However, the recording and editing techniques you'll learn will apply to all audio tracks in GarageBand— even electric guitar and bass tracks.

This lesson will show you how to set up a project for recording. Then you'll follow along with a prerecorded vocal session for an audiobook, change vocal effects to enhance the vocal sound, and edit both single and multitake regions to build a powerful narrative performance. At the end of the lesson, you'll be invited to record your own voice.

Preparing to Record Audio Tracks

In the next few exercises you'll work with some of the project properties and additional settings you need to consider before recording musical or nonmusical spoken word audio tracks. You can change the project properties later, but with audio regions—especially voice-based recordings—major changes to the project tempo will negatively affect the sound during playback. Here are a few things to consider before creating a new project that will contain audio tracks:

▶   Is the project music based or nonmusical?

▶   If the project is music based, what is the tempo? Not sure? No worries; you can tap out your project's tempo in the next exercise.

▶   If the project is nonmusical, is there a chance you'll be adding Apple Loops or other supporting music tracks later? If so, what tempo would the added music be?

▶   What microphone input are you using? Options include the built-in microphone on the computer, a USB microphone, or an external microphone connected through the computer's audio in-port.

▶   How are you monitoring (listening to) the track as you record?

In the next exercise you'll create a new project with a vocal audio track and set it up for recording audiobook narration.

Setting Project Properties

Project properties include the project tempo, time signature, and key. You can change any of these properties in the LCD display after you create a project. However, the best time to set the tempo and key is when you create a project or before you record any audio tracks.

As you may recall, Software Instrument recordings are incredibly flexible and can conform to any tempo or key change. Audio recordings, on the other hand, always sound best at their native settings—native meaning the original project properties they were recorded with. Although audio regions can adapt pretty well to minor changes to project key or tempo, big changes can affect their playback.

Rather than explain the different project properties you need to understand before recording audio tracks, let's just address them while creating a new project.

1   If you have an external microphone that you'd like to use for recording your own vocals, connect it to your computer now. If you'll be using the built-in microphone on your computer, you're all set. If you don't have a microphone, continue reading and following along.

For this project, I'm using a Blue Snowball USB microphone connected to my MacBook Pro.

2   Open GarageBand. If GarageBand is already open, choose File > New.

3   In the Project Chooser, click the New Project button to see a list of project templates.

4   Select the Empty Project template, but don't click Choose or double-click to open it yet. There are a few details about the project we must go over first.

NOTE ▸ If you accidentally created the new project, just close the project and repeat steps 3 and 4.

5 In the lower-left area of the Project Chooser, click the Details triangle to display the project properties.

▸ Tempo is pacing—the pulse or speed of the song—and it affects how the song sounds and feels. Tempo is measured by beats per minute (bpm). Software Instruments and Apple Loops automatically change tempo to match the project.

▸ Time Signature is the musical time signature used to count beats within a measure of the song and is displayed as a fraction. A song using 4/4 time means there are four beats per measure. A song using 3/4 time has only three beats per measure.

▸ Key is the musical key for the entire project. Once you set the key, all of the prerecorded loops will automatically match the project key. There are 12 different notes or keys you can set for your project.

The current settings are the default settings for each new GarageBand project. Let's take a closer look at some of the default settings before modifying the project tempo.

1 Locate the Tempo slider at the top of the project properties area. The current tempo is 120 bpm, as you can see in the bpm field.

2   Click the Key Signature pop-up menu to see the various project keys.

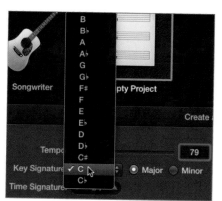

There are 12 different keys from which to choose. The default is a good key to work with, so let's leave it set to C. Radio buttons allow you to specify either major or minor. Keep the project scale set to Major.

The next project property is Time Signature, which you set by clicking the arrows to change the number of beats (or you can double-click the time signature to enter a new one).

Changing a project's time signature has no effect on the sound of a project or the regions within. Time signature is just the counting method used for beats in a measure. Different types of music use different time signatures. Most pop or rock songs use 4/4 time. If you count the beats out loud, they would be one-two-three-four, one-two-three-four. A waltz, on the other hand, uses a slower 3/4 time. The count sounds like one-two-three, one-two-three.

Let's leave the time signature at 4/4 for this project.

Since you'll be recording an audio track, you'll also need to set the audio input and output.

3   Choose an input source from the Audio Input pop-up menu. Choose Built-in Microphone if you do not have an external microphone for this lesson. Just remember to
monitor your microphone recording through headphones instead of speakers while
recording.

4   Set the Audio Output pop-up menu set to Built-in Output for now. The Built-in Output includes your computer speakers or headphone output.

NOTE ▸ If you are using external speakers connected to the computer through an audio
interface that is not connected to the Audio Out port, change the Audio Output menu
to System Setting and choose your audio interface from the system Audio preferences.

The basic project settings are finished. The last thing to set is the project tempo.

Using the Tap Tempo Button to Set the Project Tempo

How do you know what tempo the song should be? Good question. It varies based on the
genre of music. Pop songs might have a tempo of 120 bpm, whereas a hip-hop song can
be anywhere between 80 and 100 depending on the style. House, trance, and techno music
genres have much faster tempos, ranging from 125 to 150 bpm. Reggae songs tend to be
much more laid back and slower, around 70 to 80 bpm. Disco and jazz-funk typically
clock in at between 115 and 125 bpm.

All of the music you have worked with so far has had a tempo of 120 bpm. The good news
is that once the project is open you can listen to the metronome click track to hear the
current tempo. Then you can adjust it as needed. The important thing is to select a comfortable tempo for your project *before* recording audio tracks.

How do you guess the tempo of your song ahead of time, without a click track? You use
the handy Tap Tempo button to tap out the tempo you have in your head. Let's try it.

1   In your head, count one-two-three-four several times at any tempo you feel comfortable with for a song you might like to record. Pick a favorite song if that helps. Feel free to tap your foot and count out loud if that helps you count at a consistent pace.

2   Move the cursor over the Tap Tempo button. Do not click. Instead, tap lightly on your mouse or trackpad. Try tapping with the same tempo you counted in your head: one-two-three-four.

The button dims slightly with each tap to indicate it registered the tap. The Tempo field will update to match the tempo that you tap. Continue tapping the Tap Tempo button until you see a consistent range of numbers in the Tempo field.

NOTE ▶ If you click the Tap Tempo button, you'll see an average tempo based on the most recent taps.

Now that you know the general tempo you have in your head, you can set the tempo to the nearest number ending in 5 or 0. If your range is 116, 114, 117, a tempo of 115 would be a good place to start. My range was near 80 so I set my project's tempo to 80 bpm. Project tempo is whatever feels right for a project; it doesn't have to be a number that ends in 5 or 0, though most project tempos do.

3   Drag the Tempo slider or type the number for your tempo in the Tempo field. Press Return or click the Choose button to create the new project.

What the what? Instead of a new project, you see the New Track dialog.

Working with New Audio Track Settings

All GarageBand projects, even the template called Empty Project, still need at least one track. Since this project template is "empty," you get to select what type of track will be added to the project.

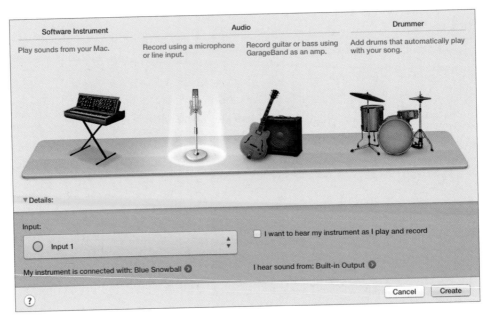

1   Click the microphone under the Audio track choices to choose an audio track with microphone or line input. Then look at the details area at the bottom of the New Track dialog.

The input and output settings you selected in the New Project dialog are displayed as statements at the bottom of the Details area.

The circled arrows next to each statement open the GarageBand preferences, where you can change the project settings.

2   Click the "I want to hear my instrument as I play and record" checkbox.

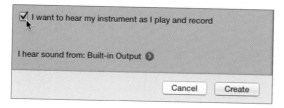

This checkbox automatically turns on the monitor settings for the new track. You can always turn track monitoring on or off using the track header controls.

3   Click the Input pop-up menu to see the options. For this project, keep the default setting of Input 1.

The Input pop-up menu lets you choose between recording mono tracks (Input 1 or Input 2) or stereo (Input 1 + 2).

NOTE ▶ Traditionally, voice-over and narration are recorded as single mono tracks. They can always be doubled on separate tracks in the timeline.

How do you know when to record mono and when to record stereo? Well, it depends on the instrument and the recording. A single instrument with only one output jack is a mono output. An instrument such as a keyboard with multiple outputs (left and right) gives you a choice of stereo (both left and right outputs) or mono (only the left output).

If you're recording a number of musicians at the same time through a mixing board or console, the signal from each musician may be routed into the mixing board as a mono input. Then the signals are mixed in the board and sent out of the mixer into the computer as a stereo signal.

You can also record a single guitar as a stereo input by changing the track settings to stereo. It just depends on what type of signal you're working with and what you're trying to accomplish.

Each track in GarageBand has two channels for audio recording and playback: Input 1 and Input 2. If you record a track in stereo, you use both channels. If you record mono, you record only Input 1 or Input 2.

> **NOTE ▶** The default mono setting is Input 1. If you are recording to two mono tracks at the same time, such as an electric guitar and USB microphone, you would set one of the mono tracks to Input 1 and the other to Input 2.

1   Click Create to create the new audio track in your new "empty" Untitled project.

If you are using the built-in microphone, you will see an Avoid feedback warning dialog. That is your signal to plug in headphones before recording. This is a default warning anytime you record with the built-in microphone and built-in output. Why? Because anytime a microphone is too close to speakers there is a risk of feedback. The simple solution is to use headphones to monitor your output while recording. If you don't have headphones, mute your computer's audio output while you record.

Your new project opens with one audio track and the Library displayed so that you can easily add a patch to your track.

2   Save the project as *My Vocal Track* in your projects folder on the desktop.

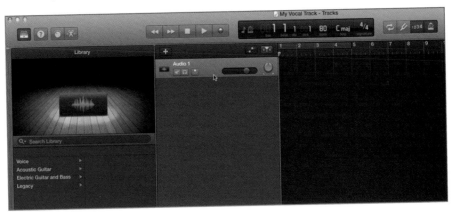

3   Find the Input Monitoring button on the Audio 1 track header. This button is orange when it is turned on. As long as the Input Monitoring button is on, you will be able to hear your track input through the computer speaker or headphones.

4   In the LCD display, locate the project tempo, key, and time signature.

5   Start playback to hear the metronome click track for the project. The click track tempo should be similar to the pace you set with the Tap Tempo button.

6   In the LCD, click the tempo (bpm) and drag upward to speed up the tempo. Then drag downward to hear the click track at a slower tempo.

   NOTE ▶ GarageBand projects can have a tempo as slow as 5 bpm and as fast as 990 bpm.

   In Lesson 6, you'll learn how to change a project's tempo within a song using the Tempo track. For now, you'll use whichever tempo you just tapped.

7   In the LCD, double-click the project tempo and type the tempo you chose using the Tap Tempo button. Stop playback.

   There is one last setting to change in the LCD: the LCD display mode. The LCD display shows either beats and project time or actual time.

   Musical projects are dependent on beats and project time to keep all of the regions in musical time with each other. For nonmusical projects, such as audiobook narration or voice-over, you can change the project to actual time.

8   Click the Display Mode pop-up and choose Time.

The LCD changes to show time in hours:minutes:seconds.frames, and the timeline ruler changes to display seconds rather than beats and measures.

9   Save the changes to the project.

That's it. You are now armed with the skills to change project settings as needed. You also know how to create a new audio track for recording vocals. At the end of the vocal exercises, you'll be invited to open this project and record your voice.

Following an Audiobook Narration Recording Session

In the next series of exercises, you'll work with a project containing numerous tracks that represent the different stages of a real-life audiobook recording and editing session. The vocal talent for this session is the award-winning poet and author Tina Sacco, who also happens to have experience as a professional voice-over artist. For this project, Tina performs the narration of her poem "Life's Flower."

1   Open the project **5-1 Audiobook Starting** and save it to the My GarageBand Projects folder on your desktop.

2 See if you can spot the following items in this project, in no particular order. If you have been following along with the lessons in the book you should have no trouble with this GarageBand seek-and-find exercise.

▶ The Library and Note Pad are both showing.

▶ The LCD display is in Time display mode.

▶ The audio track headers have Record Enable and Input Monitoring buttons showing.

▶ There are eight tracks. (These tracks represent the different stages of the recording session in chronological order, starting with the first track.)

▶ The bottom four tracks have been muted.

▶ The top two tracks have been soloed.

▶ The bottom track contains a software instrument region.

▶ The poem "Life's Flower" is on the Note Pad.

NOTE ▶ The Note Pad was used in this recording session as a prompt so that Tina could read her award-winning poem directly in the project while recording. There are three ways to add text to the Note Pad: You can type it in, copy the text from another document and paste it in, or use dictation to speak the text and it will type for you. You can turn on the dictation feature in the Edit menu. The dictation feature is especially handy if you are working on a piece of music and some lyrics pop into your head while you are crafting the song.

Now that you've seen how the project is set up, let's listen to the first audio track recording.

3   Play the project. You should hear only the audio on the top track called Audio 6.

What did you think? The performance is okay. Keep in mind it was a first take, and generally it takes the first run-through to discover everything from where the microphone should be placed to whether the input level needs improvement.

Also, this is a new audio track (just like the one you created earlier), so it has no effects or patch presets added to enhance the track. Besides listening to the dry (no reverb applied), effect-free sound of the vocal recording, how else can you tell there are no effects applied to the track? Look at the Library. If a patch were applied to the track, it would appear in the patch list for the selected track. You can also check the track's Smart Controls pane.

4   Click the Smart Controls button, or press B to see the Smart Controls for the Audio 6 track.

As suspected, the compressor switch (in the lower left of the screen controls) is turned off. Also if you check out the Ambience and Reverb Sends on the right side of the screen controls you'll see they are both dialed to the lowest setting, meaning no effect has been applied.

Thank goodness for second takes, or in this case second tracks.

TIP When recording vocals, it's best to record the tracks clean, without a lot of effects. You can always add effects later in the mixing process. When you're recording musical vocal performances, it is nice to add just enough reverb to the track to help the vocalist maintain confidence while monitoring her performance with headphones. Even the most powerful singing voices sound best with a little reverb.

5 Select the Life's Flower 1 track header.

The Library shows that a Natural Vocal patch has been applied to the track. Also, the Smart Controls indicate that the Natural Vocal patch includes both ambience and reverb. Let's hear how the Natural Vocal patch affects the sound of the recorded audio region.

6 Drag the region in the first track (Audio 6) down to the second track (Life's Flower 1).

> **NOTE ▶** Make sure that only the top two tracks are soloed so that you will hear the sound from only those tracks.

7   Play the project.

Did you hear a difference? The performance definitely sounds better with the Natural Vocal effects preset applied.

8   Unsolo the top two tracks. Solo the third track called Life's Flower 2 and the fourth track called Compressed Vocal.

9   Play the project to hear the second vocal take.

For this take, the microphone was moved closer to Tina, so her voice sounds stronger. Also applied was a Compressed Vocal patch, which helps keep the volume level of the words more even throughout the track.

The performance is great. Take a moment to listen to it with the different voice patches.

10 Play the project again. This time, during playback, select each of the different voice patches to hear how they affect the vocals. Keep an eye on the Smart Controls pane when you change patches so you can see which controls and settings have the greatest impact on the sound.

Many of these voice presets are ideal for singing performances, but don't work well for spoken narration.

11 When you are finished experimenting, select the Compressed Vocal patch and stop playback.

> **NOTE ▶** In case you were wondering why the name of the track didn't change to Compressed Vocal, or any of the other patch names when they were selected, it's because the track was manually named by the user (me) in this case. Once you type a track name, it will keep that name regardless of the selected patch.

Now let's move on to the next exercise, where you'll use the Audio Editor to clean up the sound at the beginning of the region.

Removing Parts of a Region in the Audio Editor

In this exercise you'll use the Audio Editor to select and delete the beginning of an audio region. Why not just trim the beginning of the region in the timeline? Dragging the edge of a region in the timeline works for general musical arrangement purposes, but with spoken words you need to be very precise with your editing to make sure you don't clip off the beginning or end of words. Fortunately the Audio Editor is designed for exactly the purpose it is named for—editing audio regions.

Before you edit the region, let's create a duplicate so you'll be able to compare the before and after versions of the region.

> **TIP** ▶ It's always a good idea to duplicate a recording before you start editing it so you'll have the original recording if you need it.

1   Option-drag the Lifes Flower#02 region from the third track to the empty fourth track.

> **NOTE** ▶ You may have noticed that the names of the recorded regions do not match the track names. If you recall, recorded regions take the name of the track they are recorded into. Also, the name of a region is also the name of the actual audio file. It is not a good idea to include punctuation in file names (unless the software adds them as part of a naming convention.) So, I renamed the tracks after they were recorded to include the apostrophe in "Life's Flower."

2 Unsolo the Life's Flower 2 track (the third track) so that you can hear only the Compressed Vocal track.

3 Click the Note Pad button, or press Command-Option-P to hide the Note Pad.

4 Select the Compressed Vocal track and press E to display it in the Audio Editor.

5 Press Return to move the playhead to the beginning of the timeline and editor.

6 Drag the horizontal zoom slider in the editor to the right until the editor is focused on the first five seconds of the region (0:05).

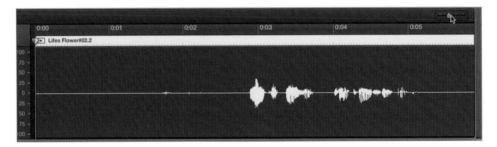

You could zoom in even further, but at this level you ought to be able to get the job done without forgetting where you are in the track.

NOTE ▶ To move the playhead in the Audio Editor, click the region headers in the editor. If you click the ruler, you will turn on the cycle area.

7 Play the beginning of the track. Listen for the nonspoken sounds consisting of distinctive clicks as Tina opens her mouth to begin speaking.

When you record someone speaking clearly and at a good volume level, you are bound to pick up additional sounds. You may not see them very well on the audio waveform, but you can sure hear them. No problem. Breath sounds are also common in voice-over and narration recordings. In this example you get to remove both at once.

There are three different tools that you can use in the Audio Editor, depending on the position of the pointer over the region in the editor:

▶ (arrow/selection tool)—The default pointer is used for selecting and for dragging a region horizontally in the editor. This tool is available when the pointer is over the upper half of the region in the editor (above the audio waveform).

▶ —The Trim tool is used for trimming regions to lengthen or shorten them. It is available only over the lower-left or lower-right edge of a region.

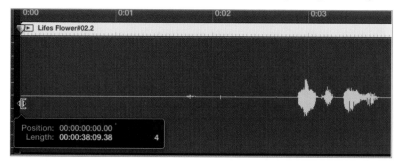

▶ —The Marquee tool is used for selecting a portion of a region and splitting it from the rest of the original region. Once you've made your selection with a marquee, you can split, delete, move, copy, or paste the new region.

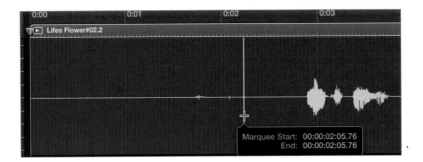

Tina's first words start just before three seconds (0:03). Your goal is to use the Marquee pointer to select a portion of the region just before she speaks. Don't worry if your selection isn't perfect. You can always trim the remaining region with the Trim tool.

8   In the editor, move the pointer just below and to the left of the largest part of the waveform just before three seconds. Click the Marquee tool to begin selection at that position. While holding down the Marquee tool, drag left to about one and a half seconds. Release the Marquee tool.

At this point, three things can happen with your selection:

▶   You can press Delete to remove the selected area from the region.

▶   You can click anywhere in the lower half of the editor to deselect the marquee (lose your selection) and make a new selection.

▶   You can click in the upper half of the selected area to turn the selection into a separate region.

For this exercise you'll go with the third option and turn the selection into a new region.

9   Click the upper half of the selected area. The selection becomes a new selected region. Press Delete.

The selected portion of the original region is no longer in the editor or the track in the timeline.

NOTE ▶ This technique is great for removing problem areas within a region while keeping the rest of the recording intact. You can also use this technique for moving, deleting, or copying and pasting smaller regions into other tracks. If the talent mispronounces a word that later they say perfectly, you can select, copy, and paste the second instance over the first.

10 In the Audio Editor, play the region that starts just before three seconds. Listen to hear if you got all of the nonverbal noise and breath out of the region with your edit.

11 If you still hear breath sound or clicks before Tina says "Life's Flower," drag the lower-left edge of the region with the Trim tool toward the right until you've cleaned up the track before her first words. If you over-trimmed your first edit and removed some of her words, you can trim toward the left to lengthen the region.

Mission accomplished. Now you can just delete the short region from the beginning of the track.

TIP ▶ When trimming dialogue or spoken words, don't trim too tightly—you may accidentally remove part of the words.

12 In the Audio Editor, select the first region at the beginning of the Compressed Vocal track. Press Delete.

13 Solo the Event Horizon track (the lowest track) and play the project to hear Tina's edited take along with a light instrumental background.

Sounds great. There are still a few extraneous noises that should be removed, but you get the idea how to do it, and that is the most important thing.

Project Tasks

Editing voice-over and narration is tedious but rewarding work. In music you can often hide things with other tracks and effects. Spoken words are less forgiving. You know what that means? It's time to get to work and clean up your track! Seriously, if you want some practice removing unwanted sounds from a track, here is your chance.

As you work, try removing as little of the region as possible. This recording was not done in a studio and therefore has some noticeable room sound (called *room tone*). Because of that, you can't leave gaps in the track or it will be audible. Instead of leaving little gaps where you remove clicks, you can either plug the gap with a piece of track that has the room tone from another area in the region, or you can pull the regions together to remove the gaps. For this track, you'll do the latter and pull the regions together. The pauses between words are part of the performance, so there is no need to remove them or tighten the spacing in this piece.

Use your new Audio Editor skills to select and delete the following:

▶ Remove the click at around :23 seconds. When finished, drag the upper half of the region on the right side of the gap until the two regions touch. Listen to make sure your edit sounds good before moving on to the next.

NOTE ▶ If you overlap the regions, only the portion of the region on the top will be audible. Since this project's LCD, Ruler, and Grid are all based on time rather than musical measures and beats, the regions do not snap to the grid lines or each other. This is very helpful for editing narration, sound effects, and other non-musical regions often based on visual cues in the Movie track.

▶ Remove the click at around :30 seconds, and then tighten the regions to remove the gap.

When you are finished, play your edited track along with the Event Horizon track to hear them together. Don't forget to save your progress.

Editing a Multitake Audio Region

In the previous exercises, you edited a single-take recording. In this exercise you'll work with a multitake region that contains three separate takes of Tina's performed narration. Multitake recordings work best for short recordings where performers can try different levels of inflection, emotion, or energy in each take.

The advantage of working with multitake regions is that all of the takes are in one convenient package. You can easily switch between takes and choose which takes you like.

What if you want to use parts of each take? You can split a multitake region right in the timeline and then choose a different take for each region. The only catch is that once you split the multitake region, you can't use the Trim tool to extend it beyond the split. No worries; if that happens, you can just delete the unused takes and the region works just like a single-take region—complete with all of the takes intact, in order, in one long take. Let's try it so you can see for yourself.

> **NOTE** ▸ If you did not complete all of the previous exercises in this lesson, open the project **5-2 Single Take Edited** and save it to your projects folder.

1   Press Y to hide the Library, if it is still showing. Press Command-Option-P, or click the Note Pad button to display the Note Pad. Since you will be listening to multiple takes, it is nice to have the poem in front of you so that you can follow the performances better.

2   Unsolo the Compressed Vocal track. Select the Multi-take region track and press S to solo the track. Unsolo the Event Horizon track for now so you can focus on the narration tracks.

3   Press Command-D to duplicate the selected track. Press Command-D again to create another duplicate track.

Notice that the duplicate tracks are both named Compressed Vocal. These tracks will take the name of whatever instrument patch is assigned to them unless you type in a new name. Because the track you duplicated had the Compressed Vocal patch, so do the new duplicate tracks. These are just work tracks for you to use for your editing, so the name is inconsequential. The new tracks are also already soloed, which is a plus for this exercise.

4   Option-drag the region in the Multi-take region track and place the duplicate in the lower compressed vocal track that you created. That way you have a backup, just in case you need it. Unsolo the track with the backup multitake region.

5   Play the project to hear Take 1 of the multitake region.

The beginning of Take 1 is good for the first few lines, but around 17 seconds (0:17) when the poem changes to the third paragraph about the fragrant rose, I'm listening for a change in inflection or stronger emotion. Luckily Tina is a pro, and since we were recording multiple takes, she read each take differently to give us more choices. Next take.

6   Click the 1 in the upper-left corner of the multitake region and choose Take 2 from the Takes menu.

7   Play Take 2 and listen for which parts you like best. Then change the Takes menu to Take 3 and evaluate that take.

For me, Take 2 has the best performance of the last three lines starting with "insig-nificant." Take 3, on the other hand, has the strongest performance of the third stanza about the rose, as well as the first line of the fourth stanza introducing the sweet baby's breath. You may have interpreted the performances differently; after all, it is poetry. However, for this exercise you can follow my lead.

8   Change the multitake region back to Take 1.

Now that you have evaluated the takes, you are ready to edit the multitake region in the timeline.

Splitting Regions in the Timeline

Previously, you split a region in the Audio Editor. In this exercise, you'll split a region in the timeline using the playhead and a keyboard shortcut (Command-T). You can also split multitake regions in the editor, but since you've already done that, you can just use the editor as a guide for positioning the playhead. First, since you'll be splitting the region in the timeline, let's zoom in a bit to make it easier to work.

1   Press Return; then zoom in to the timeline until the right edge of the multitake region almost touches the Note Pad. Make sure that both the timeline and Audio Editor Catch buttons are turned on (blue).

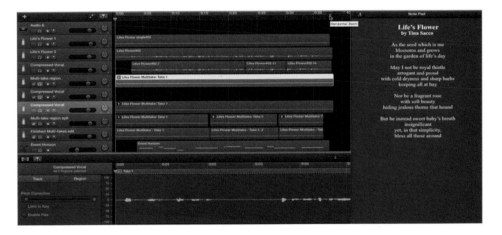

2   Play the project. Stop playback after Tina says "Keeping all at bay," around 0:17 in the time ruler.

3   Look at the playhead position in the Audio Editor. The playhead should be somewhere in the silent section of the region between 0:16 and 0:17 (around 00:16:15.00 in the LCD display). If needed, move the playhead in the Audio Editor until it is over the silent area.

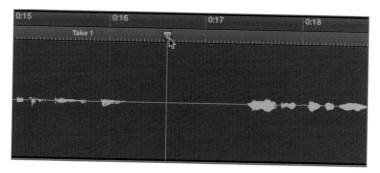

4   Click the empty track in the tracks area to deselect all regions. Then select the multitake region you want to edit. Why deselect before selecting? Because chances are the duplicate backup region or another region was also selected, and you would've edited more than one region at a time. Safety first. Once you have selected the multitake region, press Command-T, or choose Edit > Split Regions at Playhead.

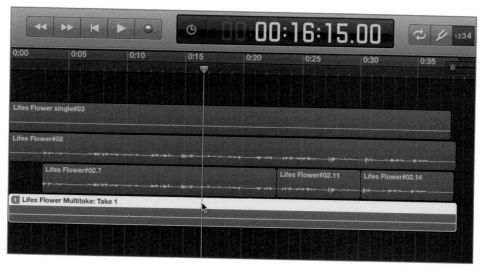

There are now two multitake regions in the track. Both regions are still showing Take 1.

5   Change the second region to Take 3.

6   Play the edit between regions to hear how they sound together.

Yikes. You can hear Tina repeat the same line at the end of the first region and the beginning of the second region. Welcome to the world of dialogue editing. Time-based recordings don't use a click track, beats, or measures to keep time, so it is rare that spoken words perfectly line up in a multitake region.

You are going to need to trim off the beginning of the Take 3 region so that it starts at 20 seconds (0:20). You can trim directly in the timeline.

7   In either the Audio Editor or timeline, try dragging the lower-left edge of the Take 3 region toward the right to trim the beginning of the region so that it starts at 20 seconds (0:20).

Didn't work? That's because you can only trim the right edge of a multitake region. You can't use the Marquee tool either. Thus, you have discovered the editing disadvantage of working with multitake regions.

You can, as you already know, split the region in the timeline, so let's do that.

8   Select the Take 3 multitake region and move the playhead to 20 seconds. Press Command-T to split the region at the playhead position.

9   Select the small Take 3 region that you just created and press Delete.

The unwanted portion of Take 3 is now out of the way.

10 In the timeline, drag the remaining Take 3 region to the left until it is close to the end of Take 1 in the Multi-take region track. To make sure there is no gap, once you have placed the regions next to each other in the timeline, check the Audio Editor to see if there is a gap between the regions. If so, drag the upper half of the Take 3 region to the left as needed until the regions touch. In the Audio Editor, swipe the visible area and adjust the horizontal zoom as needed to see the space between Multi-take regions.

TIP ▶ If you ever lose your region in the editor, simply double-click the region in the timeline twice. The first time hides the editor. The second double-click loads that region in the visible area of the editor. Also, try using the LCD and rulers in the timeline and editor as a guide.

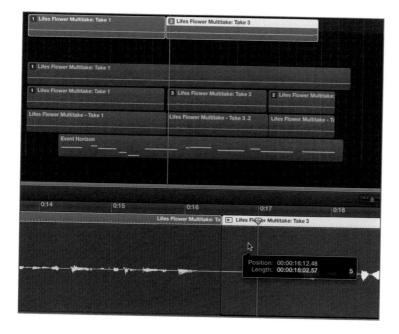

Now you can see how both the timeline and Audio Editor can be used together to edit and move a region.

11 Play the project from 10 seconds to 20 seconds to hear the edit.

It sounds okay, but the pause may be too long before Tina starts the next stanza, "Nor be a fragrant rose…." We won't know until we play the final edit with the music and hear it all in context.

12 Play the Take 3 region and pause after Tina says "sweet baby's breath" at around 28 seconds. Make sure the Take 3 region is selected, and then press Command-T to split the region.

13 Change the new Take 3 region to Take 2. Listen to the edit.

Oops. The Take 3 region ends okay, but we cut off most of the word "insignificant" at the beginning of the Take 2 region. Since the performance of that particular word is the whole reason we are cutting to Take 2 here, we need to extend the beginning of Take 2.

The only way to use the trim tools on this region is to change it from a multitake region to a single-take region.

Deleting Unused Takes from a Multitake Region

You can delete unwanted takes from a multitake region in the Takes menu. Once the takes have been deleted, the remaining take becomes a single take region that includes all of the takes in chronological order. Sound confusing? It isn't once you've seen it for yourself.

1   Drag the last region in the Multi-take region track (Take 2) down one track to the empty Compressed Vocal track you created earlier.

2   Choose Delete Unusued Takes from the Takes menu. The last region has Take 2 at the end of the name but no longer includes a Takes menu. It has transformed to a single-take, fully editable region.

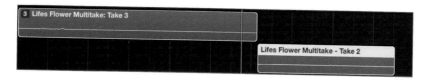

3   Zoom out of the timeline until the new region is in the middle of the tracks area with plenty of room to the right to extend the region.

4   Drag the right edge of the new region as far as you can to fully extend it. Play the region.

The region contains not only the rest of Take 2 but also the entire third take. As you learned earlier, when you delete takes from a multitake region all of the takes are still in there and accessible if needed. Pretty cool.

5   Press Command-Z or choose Edit > Undo Length Change to return the region to its former length. Feel free to adjust the timeline zoom as needed for the rest of the lesson.

6   Unsolo the Multi-take region track so you can concentrate on the Compressed Vocal track with the newly "single" region.

7   Select the newly single region in the timeline to make it easier to see in the Audio Editor. In the Audio Editor, drag the lower-left edge of the region with the Trim tool until the word "insignificant" is fully audible. Leave a little room in front of the word if possible.

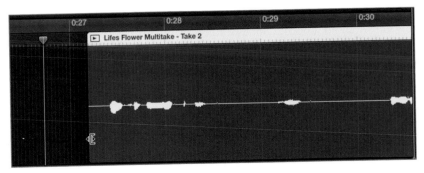

8   Once you have restored the word "insignificant" to the beginning of the region in the Compressed Vocal track, drag the region horizontally in the timeline so that it begins right after the end of the Take 3 region in the track above. Play the edit between the regions.

The edit between regions should sound seamless.

9   Solo the Event Horizon track to play it with the edited multitake regions.

10 Unsolo the tracks with multitake regions and solo the third track with the edited single-take region so you can compare the two edited versions of the poem. Tough call. They both sound great.

11 Save your finished project. If for some reason you didn't complete all of the exercises in this lesson and want to hear the finished project, open **5-3 Audiobook Finished** to hear the finished edit.

Bravo! When you are finished take a bow because you just completed some advanced dialogue editing!

> **NOTE ▸** If you'd like to contact Tina Sacco or learn more about her poetry and other writings, go to KlarkLaw.com and check out the Entertainment Representation, Featured Talent page.

Bonus Vocal Recording and Editing Exercises

If you enjoyed working with this audiobook narration project, here are four different bonus exercises you can work on at your own pace.

Using professional equipment and software ranging from film to Final Cut Pro, I've edited more than a dozen big projects from feature films to documentaries and television pilots. When it comes to editing dialogue, narration, and voice-overs, it gets easier the more you do it. Your ear becomes more tuned to subtle performance differences and nuances in the spoken words. Over time you become quicker to pick up on the mistakes that need extra work, while at the same time recognizing when something sounds believable, honest, or powerful.

Bonus Exercise 1

Using the audiobook project you've been working with throughout this lesson, make two new Compressed Vocal tracks. Edit a new version of Tina's "Life's Flower" poem using your favorite parts from all the different takes.

Bonus Exercise 2

In the audiobook project you've been working with throughout this lesson, create a new audio track, connect your mic, and record your own narrative performance of "Life's Flower." Be sure to record at least two different single takes, or two takes in a multitake region (using the cycle area to determine the length of the takes). Listen to your recordings and edit the best parts together to create a finished version.

Bonus Exercise 3

Open the My Vocal Track project that you created at the beginning of the lesson and record a short narrative piece. Read something aloud such as a newspaper article or pages from a book. Reading instructions aloud can also be fun, or even funny, depending on the instructions and tone in which you read them. Feel free to try different inflections, performances, accents, or dialects for each take. The important thing is getting used to recording vocals, and working with them afterward.

When you are finished recording, listen carefully to each take and edit as needed to create a finished piece. Feel free to add a few musical loops from the loop browser to enhance the mood, or record an original track.

Bonus Exercise 4

If you liked working with Tina Sacco's short poem "Life's Flower," she also included another poem called "Groundhog Day" that is part of her *Home for the Holidays* compilation. You'll find the recorded takes in the bonus folder in a project called 5 Groundhog Day. You'll also find a PDF (Portable Document Format) version of the poem in the bonus folder that you can open or print as needed. You can also copy the text from the PDF document and paste it into the project's Note Pad.

Listen to the different recorded takes and edit together a finished version.

Have fun.

Lesson Review

1. When you record live audio into GarageBand, the recordings appear as what type of regions, in which type of tracks?

2. Where are the project properties displayed in the GarageBand window?

3. What is the purpose of the Tap Tempo button in the New Project dialog?

4. What is the difference between splitting a region in the Audio Editor and splitting a region in the timeline?

5. Is it possible to edit a multitake region the same way you edit a single-take region?

Answers

1. When you record live audio into GarageBand, the recordings appear as audio regions, in audio tracks.

2. In the GarageBand window, you can see the project properties in the LCD display.

3. The Tap Tempo button in the New Project dialog lets you tap the tempo of a project using your mouse or trackpad to determine what tempo to set for the project.

4. Splitting a region in the timeline uses the playhead and selected tracks to determine where to split, whereas splitting a region in the Audio Editor requires selecting a portion of a region with the Marquee tool.

5. It is possible to edit a multitake region the same way you edit a single-take region. All you have to do is delete the unused takes from the multitake region.

6

Lesson Files	APTS GarageBand Book Files > Lesson 6 > 6-1 Electric Guitar Starting, 6-2 Electric Guitar Multi-take, 6-3 WahKazoo Guitar
Time	This lesson takes approximately 60 minutes to complete.
Goals	Follow an electric guitar recording session
	Explore default effects in the Smart Controls
	Work with stompboxes in the Pedalboard interface
	Listen to different electric guitar patches
	Explore Amp Designer and build a customized amp model
	Split and separate a guitar region for dynamic change
	Copy and paste a multitake region to build guitar tracks for a song
	Use the Amp Collection project template for recording guitar tracks

Working with Electric Guitars

If you play electric guitar or know a guitarist you can record, you're in luck, because GarageBand is packed with awesome features for electric guitar and bass. In this lesson, you'll learn how to create an electric guitar track, explore different electric guitar effects presets (patches), and follow a recording session with both single-take and multitake electric guitar regions. You'll also try different amps to change the sound of a recorded guitar riff, use Amp Designer to create a customized amp, and explore the Pedalboard. And, at the end of the lesson, you'll be invited to record your own electric guitar parts.

Opening the Recording Session Project

For this recording session I invited professional musician Chad Waronicki, guitarist, songwriter, and background vocalist for the funk-rap-rock band Apache Resistance.

> **MORE INFO ▶** To learn more about the band Apache Resistance, check out apacheresistance@facebook.com. Or you can see them performing onstage at Youtube.com/apacheresistance.

Not only is Chad a guitar expert, but he started out songwriting and recording with GarageBand back when he was still in high school. Since then, he has moved up to Apple Logic Pro for his recording, so he was quite surprised to work with some of the awesome new GarageBand features.

Chad brought along his Two Ply body Stratocaster with a Warmoth walnut neck as well as his Fender Blues DeVille amplifier with an assortment of stompboxes (effects pedals). But since the point of this recording session is to explore GarageBand's electric guitar presets, amps, and pedals, Chad had to leave all his extra gear in the lobby.

So, armed only with his custom electric guitar and a cable I supplied to connect it to my MacBook Pro, Chad started recording. Let's open the project and save it to your projects folder.

1   Open the project 6-1 Electric Guitar Starting.

2   Save the project in your My GarageBand Projects folder on the desktop.

Following an Electric Guitar Recording Session

This recording session started with the Amp Collection project template; you'll work with that template at the end of the lesson. Some of the tracks were deleted to make room for the recording, effects, and editing exercises.

▶   Here is a quick rundown of the project elements, in no particular order:

▶   The Library is showing.

▶   There are 14 tracks in this project.

▶   All tracks containing regions are muted except the top track, called Guitar 14.

▶   All of the audio track headers include Record Enable and Input Monitoring buttons.

▶   The bottom track, called SoCal Kit, is a Drummer track.

▶   The LCD display is in Beats & Project mode.

▶   The project properties as shown in the LCD display include a 78 bpm tempo, the key of C major, and a 4/4 time signature.

Here is a quick recap of what we did to connect the electric guitar and prepare for recording this take.

To connect Chad's electric guitar to the computer, we used a 1/4" to 1/8" cable connected to the Audio In port on my MacBook Pro.

To record a single take in the timeline, we created a new electric guitar track (named Guitar 14). In the Smart Controls inspector, we used the following settings:

Smart Controls inspector settings for Guitar 14 track

In the Guitar 14 track header, the Record Enable button was turned on (flashing red) to indicate that the track was armed to record. Also, the Input Monitoring button was on (orange) so that Chad could hear the electric guitar through his headphones.

Chad did three things before recording: He tuned his guitar using the built-in tuner in the toolbar, he set the project tempo to 78 bpm, and finally, he practiced his riff to the click track.

In this exercise, you'll follow along and listen to Chad's riff just as it sounded when he practiced and recorded the first track.

1   Start playback and listen to the region in the Guitar 14 track.

2   As you listen to the riff, see if you can tap the 78 bpm tempo along with the metronome's click track.

Trouble is, even wearing studio headphones Chad had trouble hearing the click track over the sound of his electric guitar as he practiced his riff before we started recording. Also, you may have noticed click tracks are fabulous musical timekeeping tools, but not very inspiring if you are trying to "feel" the tempo/rhythm while you record. When he asked if I could add a drum track for him to use, I suggested he try out one of GarageBand's new virtual drummer tracks.

Needless to say, Chad was so blown away by the virtual drummers that we had to stop and listen to each of the rock drummers to find one with the hard-hitting edge he was looking for. Finally, we settled on Anders, who plays grinding beats on a massive-sounding kit. If you are working with the free install, Kyle the default drummer works well too.

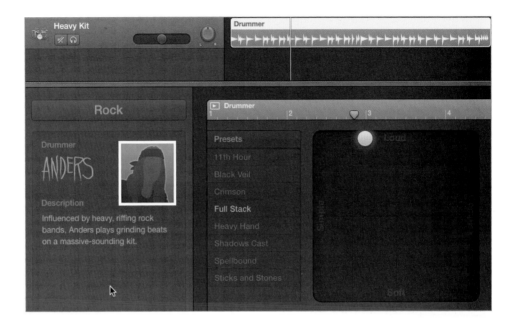

3   Click the Metronome button, or press K to turn off (kill) the metronome. Press C to turn on Cycle mode.

4   Then unmute the SoCal Kit track to hear the default Drummer track. If you have the full set of 18 Drummers and you'd like to unleash the rockin' Anders track, select the current Drummer track header and open the Drummer Editor (press E). In the Drummer Editor, click the sketch of Kyle to see all six Rock genre Drummers. Select Anders as your new Drummer. Save your project.

Whichever Drummer you are using, both Kyle and Anders work infinitely better than the lowly metronome click track.

NOTE ▶ The cycle area covers a standard 8-bar section of the song—the same length as each of the regions in the drummer track. It's no coincidence that Chad's riff is also 8 bars. The only reason the region extends beyond 8 bars is so that he could hold the last note in case we want to have it overlap another section of the song. Also, it takes a second or so to stop recording, so often single-take regions are slightly longer than the actual recorded part.

5   Start playback to hear the single-take guitar track with the drummer track. Very cool. And we are just getting started. Stop playback.

You have been listening to the guitar riff in a default electric guitar track.

Did you happen to notice that the sound of the electric guitar is very "clean" as far as electric guitar sounds go? "Clean" is another way of saying "without effects," except maybe a touch of reverb. For many musicians, recording with a "clean" sound makes it easy to focus on their performance, tempo, and the feel of the rhythm tracks.

In the next exercise you'll look at some of the effects you can add to your electric guitar tracks.

Exploring the Default Electric Guitar Track Effects

Each electric guitar track includes a complete amp model and one or more stompbox pedal effects. In the real world, amplifiers come in a variety of shapes, colors, and sizes, and each model has its own signature sound and effects.

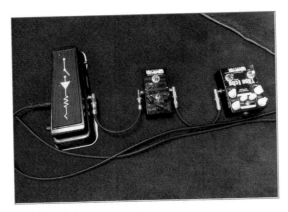

Stompboxes are so named because they're placed on the floor within reach of the musicians, so that they can quite literally stomp on them to turn them on or off as needed. A light tap of the toe also works, but is much less dramatic on stage.

GarageBand amp models and Pedalboard plug-in effects sound and respond just like the real thing—no extra equipment, cables, or stomping required. You've seen a picture of a real amp and stompboxes; now let's experiment with GarageBand's digital electric guitar effects.

1   Select the Guitar 14 track, and take a look at the instrument and patch in the Library.

Aha. Didn't I mention it sounded clean? The instrument category is Clean Guitar, and the patch is Brit and Clean. Doesn't get much cleaner than that. In case you are curious what the default Brit and Clean amp looks like, see for yourself.

At the top of the Library you'll see the track icon for the selected patch, which is an amplifier in the spotlight center stage. Not only do the GarageBand amp models simulate the sound of famous guitar amplifiers, they also look just like the real thing!

2 Press B, or click the Smart Controls button to see the default effect settings for the Clean Guitar, Brit and Clean patch.

If you look carefully at the screen controls (knobs and switches), you'll see that all of the switches are turned off except for the spring reverb. That switch is turned on, but it's set to a very light amount of reverb.

3 Start playback, and then drag up on the Spring Reverb knob to change the amount to 9 or 10. Then turn on the Echo switch and raise the amount on that one too.

You should definitely hear the change in the effects you just adjusted. Your settings may not sound good, but they will be audible.

If you want to compare your changes to the default preset settings, you can click the Compare button. When a preset has been modified, the button glows blue; when it is turned off, you see the default preset setting. Let's try it.

4 In the upper-left corner of the Smart Controls pane, click the blue Compare button to show the default settings.

5 Click the Compare button again. When it glows blue, it shows your custom settings.

> **TIP** Option-clicking any of the screen controls that are part of an instrument preset will reset them to the saved setting.

Next, you'll add some distortion and compressor effects. But wait—don't click anything yet.

You see, the effects grouped together on the left side of the Smart Controls are controlled by the amp model settings—in this case, the British Combo amp—whereas the controls grouped together in the middle are controlled by the Pedalboard plug-in. I won't tell you where the reverb is coming from. You'll discover that on your own shortly.

Using Stompboxes in the Pedalboard

The power behind the electric guitar sound is the amp model through which it plays. Amp models include both standard effects common to all amps and signature effects unique to the brand, size, or style. But when you need a little extra sound processing beyond the amp effects, you turn to stompboxes (pedals). GarageBand offers dozens of pedals through the brand-new Pedalboard. You'll find the Pedalboard in the Smart Controls pane.

1 In the upper-right corner of the Smart Controls pane, click the Pedalboard button to show the stompboxes (pedals) that come with the default track.

There is nothing subtle about the Pedalboard or the effects it contains; it takes over most of the GarageBand window real estate. You can resize the Pedalboard in a minute, but for now we'll dive in and see how Pedalboard plug-ins work. First, take in the realistic detail of the pedals and board. Notice the dent and scratches on the silver Squash Compressor. There's even nonslip carpet in the Pedal area to cushion the stompboxes.

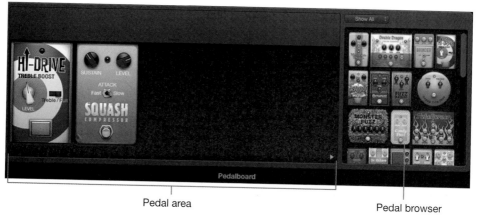

Pedal area   Pedal browser

Pedal browser—Here you can see all of the pedal effects and utilities. You can drag pedals from the browser into the Pedal area as part of the effects signal chain.

Pedal area—Here is where you set effect parameters and determine which order the effects will be in the effects chain. You can add, remove, and reorder the pedals.

The button to stomp on or off is located near the bottom of each pedal, where it would be easy to reach with a foot in the real world—or with the pointer in GarageBand. If a stompbox is turned off, the effect switch in the Smart Controls pane will also be switched off.

2   Click the On/Off switches for both pedals. A red LED light indicates that the pedals are on. Also, the corresponding switches in the screen controls area of the Smart Controls pane are in the on position.

If you are unsure which pedals correspond with which screen control you can always take a peek under the hood at the Router.

3   Move your pointer over the black horizontal panel above the pedals.

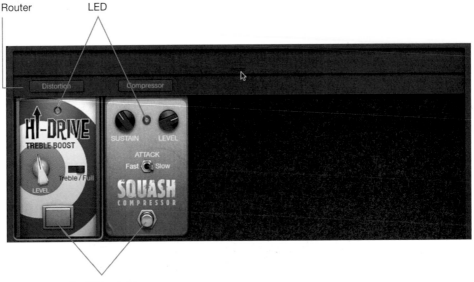

On/Off switches

The Router is where you can see which screen controls correspond with each pedal. In this example, the corresponding effects are Distortion and Compressor. Notice that both effects are now on in the screen controls because you switched them on with the stompboxes.

NOTE ▶ For advanced effects users, you can click on the effects in the Router to control signal flow to effects busses (Bus A and Bus B) available in the Pedalboard.

If you want to remove a stompbox from the Pedal area, you simply drag it off the board. You can follow Chad's lead on this one. He likes a clean spring reverb and light delay to thicken it up and give a little extra sustain. Also, typically he likes his sound a little bassier and pulls back the treble since he is the only guitarist in the band.

In other words, you're going to toss out the Hi-Drive Treble Boost pedal.

4   Drag the Hi-Drive pedal from the board and release it. The remaining pedals fill in the space to the left on the board, and the corresponding controls disappear from the Smart Controls pane.

If you decide later to add the Hi-Drive treble boost pedal, it is still available any time in the Pedal browser.

5   In the Pedal browser, click the Category pop-up to see the different pedal effect categories. These categories include Distortion, Pitch, Modulation, Delay, Filter, Dynamics, and Utility. Choose Show All from the Category pop-up if it is not already selected.

MORE INFO ▶ To learn more about the different Pedalboard plug-in effects, check out the GarageBand Help under the Help menu: GarageBand Help > Use Smart Controls > Use amps and pedals with electric guitar > Pedalboard.

You can use the Category pop-up menu to limit the pedals shown to a specific category, or choose Show All to reveal all of the effects pedals. The effects are also listed by effects category in the Smart Controls pane.

6   In the Pedal browser, select one of the stompboxes and drag it to the board. The new effect also appears in the Smart Controls pane.

NOTE ▶ If you prefer menus to dragging pedals from the Pedal browser, you can use the Manual pop-up menu in the top-left corner of the Pedalboard to manually choose plug-in effects by name. You can also use the Pedalboard Manual pop-up menu to copy, paste, load, save, and delete effects settings.

Let's resize the Pedalboard so you can get back to work in the timeline.

7   In the top-right corner of the Pedalboard, choose 50% from the View pop-up, or drag the edges to resize manually. To further reduce the size of the Pedalboard, click the disclosure triangle in the lower-right corner of the pedal area to hide the Pedal browser. Move the conveniently sized Pedalboard to the right side of the tracks area.

Ideally you will be able to see the Library, track headers, and Smart Controls pane while you test-drive four different electric guitar presets. Now that you've resized the Pedalboard, you can close or open it any time and it will remain at the current size until you change it again.

8   Start playback and listen to Chad's guitar riff with your new pedal effect applied. Turn the pedals on and off during playback to hear the sound with and without the effect.

> **TIP** Experimentation is one of the best ways to learn how effects sound together and determine which settings you like and when.

By now you probably noticed the big blue button in the upper-left corner of the Pedalboard that looks like a power button.

This is, in fact, the power button for the Pedalboard.

9   Start playback. In the upper-left corner of the Pedalboard, click the blue power button to turn it off. You can immediately hear the difference in the sound of the riff playing in the timeline. Also, visually the Pedalboard controls are dimmed on the screen controls to show they have been disabled (turned off).

10 Click the power button again to turn it back on.

You can close the Pedalboard for now, but whenever you want to see which pedal effects are in use or add a new pedal, you are ready to go.

11 Click the close button (x) in the upper-left corner of the Pedalboard to close it.

Now you know how to turn on/off, add, and remove stompboxes as well as resize, move, and close the Pedalboard. You've also seen firsthand the correlation between the screen controls and Pedalboard stompboxes. Chances are you will better understand and appreciate the different electric guitar sounds you can generate in GarageBand.

Resetting Effects to Saved Settings

It's easy to modify effect settings, so it's a good idea to learn how to get back to the original preset sound (patch). Before moving on to different electric guitar preset patches, let's take a moment to reset the default track (Guitar 14 in this project) to the saved default settings.

1 Select the Guitar 14 track header, if it is not already selected.

2 In the Library, select a different Clean Guitar patch, such as Amazing Tweed or Chicken Pickin'. Since you have a new instrument patch loaded, you might as well listen to it. Play a few bars of the riff with the new patch to hear the difference.

Whenever you select an instrument patch for a track, it changes all of the effects applied to that track accordingly.

3   Select the Brit and Clean patch to reset the effects to the original default settings. Play a few bars to hear the "clean" default guitar again.

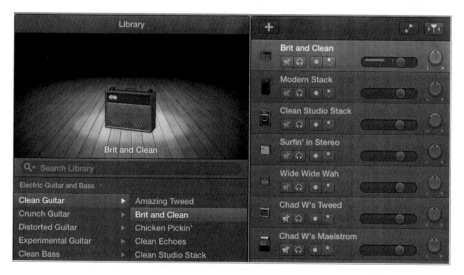

The track should sound familiar. The only difference is that the track name has changed to Brit and Clean. As a new track default, the track comes with a generic name; in this project it was Guitar 14. Once you go through the trouble of selecting a patch and changing the sound, the track names update accordingly.

Moving a Region to Different Tracks to Change Effects Patches

Time to test-drive some of the electric guitar presets already in the timeline to hear the dramatic difference between them. While you're at it, you can glance at the library to see which amp models are used for each effect, or show the Pedalboard to see the current pedal effects chain.

Let's move the guitar region to some of the empty tracks to hear how the riff sounds with different guitar patches. If you select the track header for the new track containing the region, you'll see the Smart Controls settings. Oh, and just for fun, one of the tracks has a bass guitar amp model and sound. You'll figure it out, because it will be identified as such in the Library, and there won't be a Pedalboard for the track.

1   Start playback and drag the single-take region down one track to hear the Modern Stack sound.

There will be a slight delay after you move the region to a new track before the sound switches to the new effects preset.

2   Click the track header for the Modern Stack track to see its screen controls and the preset in the Library.

3   Drag the region to the third stack called Clean Studio Stack; then click the track header to see the related patch and controls. You may have noticed it also sounds very clean. It should—all of the effects are turned off, and it is, after all, called Clean Studio Stack. You can modify the sound later, but for now, keep going to the next track.

4 Drag the region to the fourth track called Surfin' in Stereo, and click the track. Totally tubular, dude! The patch transformed Chad's riff right into a vintage surf movie soundtrack riff.

Check out the screen controls. The only effects that are turned on are Tremolo and Reverb. That means the surf sound is coming from some gnarly stompbox effects.

5 Click the Pedalboard button in the Smart Controls. Continue playback. Hover your pointer over the Router panel to see the Router effects in the chain.

Interesting. There are three stompboxes, but only Tremolo is turned on, as indicated by the red LED light. That means the other pedals are in place to further enhance the surf sound as needed.

6   Click the on switches for the Overdrive and Delay effects to hear all three pedals in action. Definitely a much edgier surf sound. Close the Pedalboard.

7   Start playback if needed and move the region to the last test track, Wide Wide Wah. Now that's a serious heavy metal sound that Anders the virtual drummer would appreciate.

A sound that big must have a massive amp. Take a look at the Track icon in the Library.

Wait…that little thing creating such a monster sound? Really? So the amp must be getting a lot of help from the Pedalboard.

8   Open the Pedalboard. Okay. That explains a lot. Four stompboxes. Yes, there are four—you have to drag the horizontal slider at the bottom of the pedal area to see them all.

9   Stop playback and close the Pedalboard.

Now that you've had a taste of the electric guitar patches and stompbox sounds you can generate in GarageBand, let's look at the last piece of the effects puzzle: the amps.

Exploring Amp Designer

Which guitar amp to use depends on the musician's style, as well as the venue where they will perform. The use of effects is just as subjective, and as with musical styles, everybody has their favorites.

When Chad is performing with his band, he typically travels with two different guitar amplifiers: a ValveTrain Trenton and a Fender Blues DeVille, depending on the size of the event.

In this exercise you'll explore the Amp Designer interface so you'll understand the various parameter areas and know how to change or customize amp models.

1   Drag the single-take riff you've been working with to the top track, now called Brit and Clean. Select the Brit and Clean header if it is not already selected.

2 Take a look at the Brit and Clean amp icon in the Library. You are about to get a much closer look at the default amp.

3 In the top-right corner of the Smart Controls pane, click the Amp Designer button. Amp Designer opens with a much larger, and realistic, version of the current Brit and Clean amp model. Feel free to resize the Amp Designer interface as needed.

Amp parameters

Effects parameters

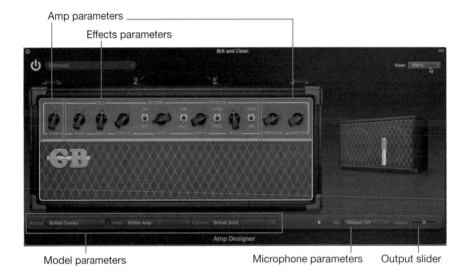

Model parameters   Microphone parameters   Output slider

Hello, British Combo! What you are looking at is the British Combo complete amp model used for the default Brit and Clean sound. Each complete amp model includes an amp, a speaker cabinet, an EQ preset, and a microphone that re-creates a well-known guitar amp sound.

The Amp Designer plug-in has the following parameter areas:

Model parameters—These are the pop-up menus in the black bar at the bottom of the Amp Designer interface that are used to choose a complete amp model, including an amplifier, a cabinet, an EQ type, and a microphone.

Amp parameters—You'll find these knobs on both ends of the knob section; they are used to set an amp's input gain, presence, and master level.

Effects parameters—These are in the center of the knobs section and control the integrated effects.

Microphone parameters—You'll find these parameters on the right side of the interface. You can use them to select the type of microphone and the position of the microphone that captures the amplifier and cabinet sound.

Output slider—This slider in the lower-right corner of the interface controls the final volume level for the Amp Designer's output. This is not the same as the Master Control knob on the amp, which is used for both sound design and controlling the level of the amp section.

Let's try some of the different parameter areas to see how they work together to complete the overall sound of the amp model. You can choose different complete amp models in the Model pop-up menu in the lower-left corner of the Amp Designer interface.

4   Start playback to hear the Brit and Clean default sound.

NOTE ▸ You don't have to see the timeline to play it. As long as Cycle mode is on, the riff will play indefinitely until you stop playback.

5   Click the Model pop-up to see all 25 complete amp models. Select the Boutique Retro Combo to see a completely different type of amp model.

Nifty look and sound. Next.

6   Select a different amp model, or go ahead and try them all. When you are finished, select the Large Tweed Combo and stop playback.

Does this amp model look familiar? There is a picture of an actual amp just like this (the Fender Blues DeVille) at the beginning of the lesson.

Let's reduce the size of the interface to focus on the Model parameters and knobs area of Amp Designer. Then you can try out some of the parameter areas to see how they work together to complete the overall sound of the amp model.

7   Click the disclosure triangle at the bottom of the Amp Designer, just to the left of the Mic pop-up. The Amp Designer window reduces to just a small interface with all of the essential parameters and controls, without showing the amp, cabinet, and mic position.

WARNING ▶ The Master level knob can produce extremely loud output that—just like in the real world—can cause damage to speakers or hearing. Always start with a low Master knob setting, and then slowly increase it as needed.

Compare the knobs area in Amp Designer to the knobs on the top of Chad's amp. Same tweed, same cabinet, same knobs (just in different placement).

The Amplifier parameters are:

Gain—This knob sets the amount of preamplification that is added to the input signal. Basically, it raises the level of the guitar sound on its way from the guitar into the amp. Hence the name preamplification.

Presence—This knob adjusts the ultra-high frequency range that is above the range of the Treble control. The Presence levels affect only the Master output as controlled by the Master knob.

Master—You can turn this knob to set the output volume of the amplifier signal sent to the cabinet.

8   Drag the reduced Amp Designer so it is directly above the Smart Controls pane.

9   Change the Model pop-up to British Combo. The Amp Designer knobs area matches the screen controls for the track. Coincidence? I think not. Clearly they are meant to go together like two presets in a pane. Click the big blue power button to turn off Amp Designer.

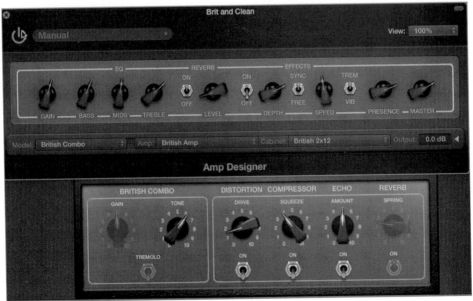

The Gain and Reverb screen controls are disabled (dimmed). Now you know where the touch of reverb was coming from in the default electric guitar patch.

NOTE ▶ All amp models include Reverb, even if the real-life amp on which the model is based does not include reverb. Reverb can be used independently or added to the Tremolo or Vibrato effect.

10 Click the power button on Amp Designer again to turn it back on.

Now that Reverb is back on, why not try a few of the different reverb sounds available in Amp Designer?

11 Above the center of the knobs area on Amp Designer, click the word REVERB to see the Reverb pop-up menu.

12 Start playback and try each of the choices in the Reverb pop-up. When you are finished, set the Reverb pop-up back to Simple Spring.

13 Click the EQ pop-up menu (above the Bass, Mids, and Treble knobs) to see the various EQ presets.

14 Start playback and try each of the different EQ presets in the EQ pop-up to hear how they sound with the current amp model. When you are finished, set the EQ pop-up back to British Bright. Stop playback.

15 Click the disclosure triangle next to the Mic pop-up menu to display the entire Amp Designer interface.

As you can see, Amp Designer is an exciting way to get the look, feel, and sound of well-known amps.

Building and Saving a Custom Amp Model

It wasn't that long ago that the only way to make your guitar sound like it was playing through a famous amplifier was to use the famous amplifiers. I know, because I played keyboards in many bands that rehearsed and recorded music in actual garages. So the idea that the GarageBand amp models can emulate well-known amplifier sounds is truly amazing.

The processed sound of a particular electric guitar and amp combo adds character and personality to a song and can be almost as important as the performance itself. Since the introduction of the electric guitar in 1931, popular bands from all genres and generations have developed their signature sounds around their electric guitars in addition to their lead vocals.

If the preset amp models let you sound like famous guitar players from your favorite bands, why would you want to change anything? Sometimes, sounding like everyone else makes it difficult to get noticed—regardless of your level of talent. Creating a fresh sound is one way to separate your music from everyone else out there. Keep in mind, a fresh sound should also work with your music, not against it.

In this exercise you'll start with a complete amp model; then you'll use pop-up menus to change the amplifier, cabinet, EQ type, and mic placement. When you are finished, you'll save your custom amp model so that you can use it on future projects or other tracks in this project.

1 In the Model pop-up choose an amp model to start with. Choose whichever model you like; just remember it will look and sound completely different when you are finished customizing it.

Now you are going to totally rebuild it into a custom amp.

2   Choose an amplifier from the Amp pop-up. If you'd like to hear how the various amps sound, start playback and listen to their sounds.

3   Choose a cabinet from the Cabinet pop-up. The cabinet will determine the number and type of speakers as well as the size of the amp.

MORE INFO ▶ If you want to learn more about the types of amp models, amps, cabinets, and EQ, check out the Smart Controls > Amp Designer section of the GarageBand Help.

4   Click the Mic pop-up menu to show the seven types of microphones available.

Although there are seven mic models, there are only three primary types:

▶ **Condensor microphones**—These have a fine, well-balanced sound and are often used in high-end studio recording.

▶ **Dynamic microphones**—These mics sound brighter and more cutting with boosted mid-range and softer low-mid frequencies. They are popular for rock guitar tones to help the sound stand out when mixed with other tracks.

▶ **Ribbon 121**—This is a type of dynamic microphone that delivers a bright yet warm sound. It's popular for rock, crunch, and clean guitar tones.

5 Make a choice from the Mic pop-up menu. Move the pointer toward the mic image (above the Mic pop-up area) to see the mic placement grid. Drag the white dot—representing the mic—in the grid to change the mic placement in front of the speaker.

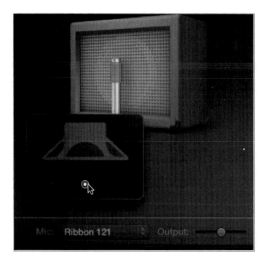

Your amp model is nearly complete. All that's left is to adjust the Reverb and EQ settings.

6 On the amp knobs area, click the EQ pop-up menu and select an EQ style that fits your customized amp model.

7 Choose a type of reverb from the Reverb pop-up. Remember, this is the default guitar track you are modifying, so the reverb may be limited. Drag the Level knob in the reverb area in the middle of the knobs area on the amp.

8 When you are finished, stop playback.

Time to save your customized amp model. You can save your amp settings in the Settings pop-up menu in the top left of the Amp Designer interface.

9 Click the Settings pop-up menu and select Save As. Do not select Save As Default or your setting will be the new default setting—not that it isn't good enough, but for now, let's just save the setting so you can use it in future projects.

10 In the Save Setting As dialog, type your first name and something that describes the amp. In this example the cabinet I used was called Sunshine 1x12 so I couldn't resist including Sunshine in the name. Do not change the location for the saved settings. As long as they save into the Amp Designer folder, you will be able to recall them any time you are using Amp Designer on the current computer. Click Save.

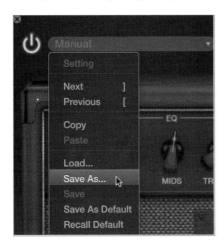

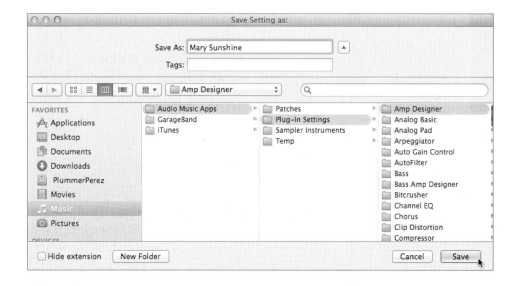

NOTE ▶ You can save settings in GarageBand for any of the Smart Control effects, including arpeggiator, amps, and stompboxes. The saved settings are on your computer under Music > Audio Music Apps > Plug-in Settings. If you use more than one computer for GarageBand, you can move your saved settings—just be sure to place them in the correct folder.

The Settings pop-up menu at the top of the interface now shows the name of your custom amp model.

11 Click the Settings pop-up menu to see your saved amp model in the list near the bottom of the menu.

You can use this menu to load any of the electric guitar instrument patches from the Library. The patches are organized in three submenus—Clean, Crunch, and Distorted—just like the Library. Select a patch from one of the submenus to load it in Amp Designer.

The amp model for whichever patch you selected automatically loads in Amp Designer and is ready for playback.

12 Start playback to hear the new patch; then close Amp Designer. Stop playback, and press B to hide the Smart Controls pane.

The amp model for the patch you selected is loaded in Amp Designer and ready to play. Now that you've experimented with electric guitar amps, screen controls, and stompboxes, it's time to get back to the timeline and put the electric guitar effects to work.

Doubling a Guitar Track

One of the most common tricks when recording electric guitars is to double the guitar part to fatten the sound. In this exercise you'll double Chad's riff and then pan the tracks left and right so it sounds like different players for each part.

1   Drag the single take of Chad's riff to the Clean Studio Stack track.

2   Option-drag the same region down one track to the Surfin' in Stereo track.

3   Start playback.

The two sounds work well together. You can try different patches later; the idea is that you have created a different sound by doubling the guitar part. This technique also works well with an acoustic guitar patch and electric guitar patch for the two tracks.

To separate the doubled tracks so that they sound like two different players, you can drag the pan dial up, to pan the sound left—or down, to pan the sound right. A little panning goes a long way. You'll learn more about panning tracks in Lesson 8, "Mixing Music and Adding EQ Effects."

4   In the Clean Studio Stack track header, click the Pan knob and drag down slowly until the Pan overlay says –25 (25 left).

5   Drag up slowly on the Surfin' in Stereo track Pan knob until the overlay shows +25 (25 right).

6   Play the tracks to see if you can hear the acoustic separation of the instruments now that one is more to the left and the other more to the right. Stop playback.

As you can see, it takes only a few minutes to double a guitar track, but it can make a big difference in the overall sound in a finished mix.

Splitting a Guitar Region to Create Dynamic Change

Another electric guitar effects trick is to change patches in the middle of a song, or even in the middle of a section of the song to change the song's dynamic. Dynamic changes are changes in volume within a song. An example of a dynamic change would be a song that starts out with a light piano instrumental intro, and then kicks into full-throttle rock in the verse or chorus.

In this exercise you'll split the guitar riff region and place half on one track and half on the other so that the dynamic jumps from one sound to the other. Then you'll extend one region so that the two guitar parts overlap to make the edit less abrupt.

So what kind of dynamic change are we going for? Let's follow Chad's lead and create a dynamic he likes to use on stage. In his words, he likes to make the dynamic go from fun and light-hearted to kicking in the door.

Let's play the finished version to hear Chad's dynamic change.

1   Solo the Chad W's Tweed track. Then, solo the Chad W's Maelstrom track.

2   Play the project and see if Chad achieved the dynamic change he was going for.

What did you think? I'd say mission accomplished. Now it's your turn to create the same effect.

3   Unsolo both of the tracks you just listened to. Directly below those tracks are two empty tracks with the same guitar patches. Solo the empty Amazing Tweed and Maelstrom tracks.

Let's move the empty tracks that you'll be working with up to the position above the Wide Wide Wah track. To reposition a track, you drag the empty space in the track's header.

4   Drag the empty Amazing Tweed track up to the position above Wide Wide Wah. Drag the empty Maelstrom track up to the position above Wide Wide Wah.

5   Drag the region in the Surfin' in Stereo track down into the empty Amazing Tweed track.

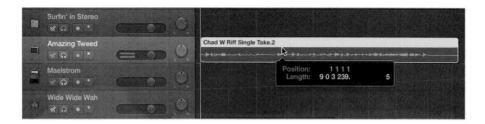

You can split an electric guitar region in the timeline the same as you split an audio region in Lesson 5. Just remember, to split a region in the timeline it has to be selected, and the playhead needs to be in the position where you'd like to make the split.

6   Select the region in the Amazing Tweed track, if it is not already selected. Move the playhead to bar 5. Press Command-T.

The region splits at bar 5.

7   Drag the second region in the Amazing Tweed track down to the Maelstrom track.

8   Turn off Cycle mode. Listen to your edit to hear the dynamic change at bar 5.

9   Drag the right edge of the region in the Amazing Tweed track and extend it one mea-
     sure to bar 6. Solo the Heavy Kit drummer track and listen to your finished edit.

10   Save your project.

That's it. You have successfully split an audio region and moved the second half to another
track to create an interesting dynamic.

Preparing the Project

Before moving on to the next exercise, let's do a little housekeeping to make sure the right
tracks are audible:

1   Unsolo the Amazing Tweed and Maelstrom tracks.

2   Unsolo the drummer track.

3   Solo the Razor Face track. It contains a region called Chad W Riff Multitake2.

4   Press Y, or click the Library button to hide the Library.

5   Adjust the horizontal zoom level in the timeline as needed using the slider (or by
     pressing Command-Right Arrow/Command-Left Arrow) until you can see from bar
     1 to bar 26 in the ruler. You can display beyond bar 26 if you like, but just make sure
     bar 26 is included in the visible portion of the tracks area.

     Perfect. Now the project is ready for the next exercise.

Working with Multiple Takes Electric Guitar Regions

You already have experience working with multitake regions. In Lesson 4, "Recording and Editing Software Instruments," you recorded a multitake Software Instrument bass part. In Lesson 5, "Recording and Editing Audio Tracks," you edited a multitake audio region that was nonmusical spoken words. Now you are going to work with an electric guitar multitake audio region. Since it is a music-based audio region, performed by a professional musician, you should be able to split the region at any bar and switch takes seamlessly.

For this exercise you will first listen to both takes of the guitar riff. Both takes sound great; they're just different variations of the same riff. That means to build the guitar track for a song, you will simply copy and paste the multitake region and alternate takes. Along the way you'll also double, overlap, and split some of the multitake regions to create the finished electric guitar tracks.

> NOTE ▶ If you didn't complete all of the previous exercises in this lesson, open the project **6-2 Electric Guitar Multi-take** and save it to your project folder on the desktop.

1   Start playback and listen to Take 1 of the multitake guitar region in the Razor Face track.

You probably noticed that Take 1 is a different riff than you have been working with, but it still follows the same groove and feel.

2   Select Take 2 from the Takes menu in the Chad W Riff Multitake2 region. Listen to the track.

This ought to sound familiar. Take 2 is a different recording of the riff you were working with in the previous exercises. Because the takes are different riffs, you can alternate them for different parts of the song, or you can combine them to create a more complex guitar section for the song.

Copying and Pasting Regions in the Timeline

You can copy and paste regions in the timeline the same way you copy text in a document. For this exercise you will copy the multitake region and paste it twice into the same track so you'll have a total of three identical multitake regions in the Razor Face track.

1 Select the Razor Face track header. This will select both the track and the multitake region in the track. Press Command-C, or choose Edit > Copy.

2 Move the playhead to bar 9 and press Command-V or choose Edit > Paste.

The multitake region is pasted into the selected track starting at the playhead position (bar 9). Notice that the playhead is positioned at the end of the newly pasted region. That means you can immediately paste another region without the need to move the playhead.

3 Press Command-V or choose Edit > Paste.

There should now be three identical multitake regions arranged back to back in the Razor Face track.

NOTE ▶ If for any reason you copied the wrong region or pasted it into the incorrect track or position, just press Command-Z or choose Edit > Undo and try the steps again. Remember, Copy always copies selected regions, and Paste always pastes regions into the selected track starting at the playhead position.

4 Save your progress.

Now the track is ready to edit, and you can create a varied electric guitar track for a song.

Project Tasks

It's your turn to work with some of the skills that you've learned so far to choose takes, alternate takes, and split the multitake region to create an interesting guitar part for the song.

You have two tracks to work with: the Razor Face track, which contains the multitake regions, and the empty guitar track below.

Start by using a full take for the first two 8-bar regions. For the last 8 bars, split the multitake region to alternate parts once or twice. Also, feel free to double the part at the end for a big finish.

Feel free to use the edited multitake tracks as a guide. The edited version is in the two tracks directly above the drummer track.

When you are finished editing the guitar parts, solo the drummer track to hear how the virtual drummer varies the drum track to go with the different guitar parts.

Finally, if you'd like, you can change the guitar patches for one or both of the multitake tracks to change the overall sound.

When you are finished, listen to your finished tracks; then save your project.

Recording Electric Guitar Tracks—Without a Guitar

Not everyone has an electric guitar, or a player skilled enough to perform the parts you need for a song. No worries. If you (or someone you know) can hum or sing the electric guitar part you need, you're all set. Really.

1   Open the project **6-3 WahKazoo Guitar** and save it to your projects folder.

The project opens with five tracks. The first three tracks are electric guitar tracks with heavy processing effects. The fourth track is a Natural vocals track. The fifth track is a drummer track playing along to the mystery guitar performance.

2   Play the project to hear the faux-guitar tracks.

NOTE ▸ These electric guitar performances were recorded by a novice musician who has never played guitar of any kind. Also the various performances were not always in time with the drummer, so I used the Groove Track to improve the timing. You'll learn how to use the Groove Track to fix the timing of tracks in Lesson 7.

3   Solo the bottom two tracks to hear the Clean - Wah and Kazoo track with the SoCal Kit. Play the project again to hear the clean recordings.

It's okay to laugh—I did. The musician, my seven-year-old daughter Katie, took her recording very seriously. As you can see in the pictures, she performed these (and many other) guitar parts using a $1.25 kazoo and her voice singing "Wah and Wow" sounds.

Katie used the built-in microphone to record both the kazoo and vocals. Kazoos make excellent faux-electric guitars because of the vibrations and range of the sound. If you don't have a kazoo, a fine-toothed comb and a piece of paper will also do the trick.

4   Unsolo the lower tracks and mute the Clean - Wah and Kazoo track. Play the project once more just to hear the difference.

This may not be a perfect performance, but I've heard adults record vocal guitar parts that were spot-on to famous guitar riffs and solos. The point of this exercise is to demonstrate that you can indeed fake electric guitar parts as needed. You can always re-record with a real guitar later. This is also useful if you just want to record a basic guitar track so you can practice with effects later.

Recording Your Own Electric Guitar Tracks

If you're ready to record electric guitar tracks, a great place to start is the Amp Collection project template. In this exercise you'll create a new project. Then you'll set up a track for recording. You'll also click the Tuner so you know how to tune your guitar right in the GarageBand window.

1   Open GarageBand. If it's already open, choose File > New.

2   In the Project Chooser, click the New Project button to see a list of project templates.

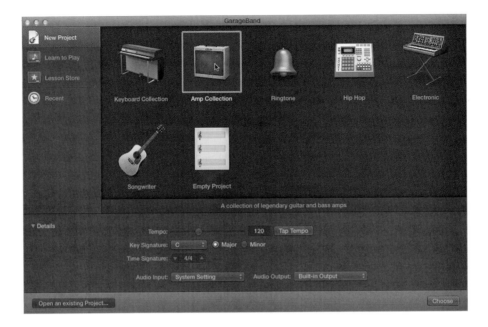

3   Double-click the Amp Collection button to automatically open the project template.

4   Save the project as *My Electric Guitar* to your My GarageBand Projects folder.

The project opens with 15 electric guitar and bass tracks ready to test-drive with your electric guitar. Notice that the first track is the default electric guitar patch Brit and Clean.

5   If you are planning to record your guitar, connect it to the computer now. If you are going to record the guitar using the built-in microphone, you're all set.

6   Select the Brit and Clean track header, if it's not already selected.

7   In the Smart Controls pane, click the Inspector button (i).

The track inspector shows the different recording information you need to set prior to recording to that track.

8   In the Smart Controls inspector, click the Monitoring button to turn it on. It will glow orange once turned on. The Monitoring button in the track header is on now as well.

NOTE ▶ If you are working with a Mac with a built-in microphone configured as the current audio input device, you may hear static or yourself when the Monitoring button is turned on, which could cause feedback. Feel free to turn off the Monitoring button if necessary.

If GarageBand detects feedback, you'll see an alert dialog with the option to change the current setting. This alert is part of the built-in feedback protection that is the default whenever you monitor recordings.

9   Select the Feedback Protection checkbox in the inspector.

10   Turn off the Input Monitoring button if you are not planning to record a guitar part at this time.

While you are looking at the inspector, take a moment to set your Input Source and Recording Level settings.

11   Click the Mono/Stereo button (it looks like a circle) to change the track input from mono to stereo (it looks like two circles linked).

Mono input   Stereo input

12   Click the Mono/Stereo button again to change the input back to mono.

13   Click the Input pop-up and select the appropriate input for your guitar: built-in, audio-in port, or an audio interface that you have connected to the computer.

14 If you have an electric guitar or microphone connected to the computer, play a few notes and adjust the Recording Level slider as necessary.

NOTE ▶ If you don't hear your guitar, make sure the volume is turned up on your instrument and that the input settings in your Mac Sound preferences are set for the correct input.

MORE INFO ▶ To learn more about connecting your guitar to your Mac, see "Connecting Instruments to the Mac" in Bonus Lesson 1, "Learning to Play Piano and Guitar with GarageBand." You can also find detailed information about connecting your electric guitar or instrument to the computer as well as the input settings for your connection in GarageBand Help > GarageBand Basics > Connect. You can find the bonus lesson online on the same page as the lesson files.

If you're going to be recording to more than one track, you'll need to use the Record Enable button.

15 Choose Track > Track Header > Show Record Enable Button.

The Record Enable button appears in all the track headers. The selected track will show a red dot to indicate that track is selected.

16 Click the Record Enable button. It will flash red to show it is armed and ready to record to that track.

The last two steps are tune and tempo. You need to tune your instrument and set the project tempo.

17 Click the Tuner button in the toolbar next to the Cycle button.

The built-in tuner window works just like a standalone digital tuner. If the note is too sharp or too flat, it will be orange. Green means the note is in tune.

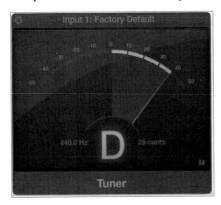

18 When you are finished tuning, close the tuner window, or click the Tuner button.

19 Start playback and listen to the click track. Drag up or down on the tempo in the LCD to raise or lower it accordingly. You can also double-click the tempo in the LCD display and type in a new tempo.

That's it. Your track is armed, your instrument tuned, and the tempo set, and you are ready to record. For single-take recording, click Record or press R to start recording at the playhead position. For recording multiple takes, set a cycle area for the length of the takes, and then start recording.

Remember, you can always change the track's instrument patch and add effects after you record.

Review Questions

1. If a guitar track is "clean," what does that mean?

2. In which part of the GarageBand window can you access the screen controls, Pedal board, and Amp Designer?

3. How do you know if a stompbox on the Pedalboard is turned on?

4. What are the four things that make a complete amp model in Amp Designer?

5. If you change a song's dynamic, what did you change?

6. Where is the tuner in the GarageBand window?

7. What button must be turned on in the track header to hear your instrument as you record?

Answers

1. A "clean" guitar track has no effects except a little reverb.

2. In the GarageBand window, you can access the screen controls, Pedalboard, and Amp Designer in the Smart Controls pane.

3. When a stompbox on the Pedalboard is turned on, the LED is red.

4. A complete amp model in Amp Designer includes an amplifier, cabinet, EQ preset, and microphone.

5. Dynamic changes in a song are changes in the volume level.

6. In the GarageBand window you can show or hide the Tuner by clicking the Tuner button in the toolbar.

7. To hear the track input as you record, you need to turn on the Monitoring button.

7

Lesson Files   APTS GarageBand Book Files > Lesson 7 > 7-1 Groove Match, 7-2 Drummer Follow, 7-3 Recording Beats, 7-4 Beats for Loops, 7-5 Beats and Tempo, 7-6 MP Crazy Beat

Time   This lesson takes approximately 45 minutes to complete.

Goals   Control timing with a groove track

Have a drummer region follow the bass track

Record multipass drum beats

Trim and fix recorded regions to make them loop ready

Add loops to the Loop Library

Make tempo changes in a project with the tempo track

Creating Drum and Percussion Tracks

Drum and percussion tracks create the heartbeat of your music. In this lesson you'll work with four types of drum and percussion tracks: a drummer track, a drum machine with arpeggiator, Apple Loops, and audio recordings of noninstrumental percussion such as stomps, claps, and the sound of a dog walking through leaves.

First you'll create a drummer track and use it to instantly fix the groove (or timing) of all the other tracks in a song. Then you'll use the Follow feature to make the drummer performance follow a bass track. In the third project, you'll record your own hip-hop beat using a MIDI drum machine with the arpeggiator and multipass recording. Once your beat is recorded, you'll fix the timing and turn it into a loop. When your loop is finished, you'll use Flex Time editing to fix a recording of stomping and clapping and turn it into a loop as well.

The last two tasks you'll explore are adding your loops to the Loop Library and creating a complex hip-hop beats project with your loops and automation with tempo control points on the tempo track.

Control Timing with Groove Tracks

Prepare yourself for a very cool exercise. You are about to use a drummer track to instantly control the timing of all the other tracks. What sounds too good to be true as you'll hear for yourself in a minute—is groove matching. This feature goes way beyond what you might expect from GarageBand. Truth is, the powerful Flex Time analysis used to make groove matching possible came from Logic Pro, Apple's professional music recording software. The good news for GarageBand users is that all the work is done for you.

What is groove matching? Well, it's a more advanced form of quantizing the music that considers the groove (meter, pacing, and feel) of a selected groove track and matches the other tracks to it. Best of all, it works with both Software Instrument and Real Instrument recordings. In this exercise, you'll use a drummer track to correct six other tracks that might otherwise be unusable.

1   Open the project **7-1 Groove Match**, and save it to the My GarageBand Projects folder.

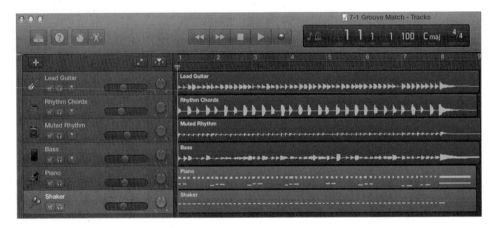

2   Play the project once.

You know the phrase "marching to the beat of a different drummer?" Well, in this case it sounds like each track was playing to a different drummer, or more likely no drummer at all. Even those of you without a musical background probably noticed that this song is a timing disaster.

Whether these parts were recorded with a click track or live drummer, none of them are in time with each other. Without a common groove, these tracks are unusable.

The good news is you can fix this musical disaster in three steps. You'll start by creating a new drummer track to control the timing of the other tracks.

3 Select the lowest track if it is not already selected. Click the Add Track button, or choose Track > New Track. In the New Track dialog, double-click the Drummer icon to create a new drummer track.

A new SoCal drummer track appears below the Shaker track. The Drummer Editor and Library are also displayed. You won't need the Library, metronome, or Drummer Editor for this exercise.

4 Press Y to hide the Library, press K to turn off the metronome, and then press E to hide the editor. Play the project to hear whether any improvement results in the SoCal Drummer track.

Nope. The drummer part is in perfect time, but the other tracks are still way out of the pocket.

NOTE ▶ "Out of pocket," "Out of the pocket," or "Not in the pocket" are polite ways for a musician or music producer to say that a track or performance does not quite fit the groove of the song. In this case, the tracks are so far out of whack they sound like an acoustic train wreck.

In the old days, you might as well have rubbed a lamp and hoped for a genie to salvage those tracks. Otherwise, you had no choice but to re-record them. Fortunately, the groove tracks in GarageBand can perform their own magic—without the genie.

Before you continue, it's a good idea to decide which track best represents the feel of your song. Drummer tracks are usually a safe bet, but you might also choose a track that could stand alone. Do you have a track that a vocalist could sing along to "unplugged"? In that case, the rhythm guitar or a lead piano part would work. For this song, the drummer track you just created is the only one that you would want to use to control the other tracks.

5   Control-click (or right-click) the SoCal track header; then choose Track Header Components > Show Groove Track from the shortcut menu.

6   Hold the pointer over the left edge of the SoCal track header. Click the star on the left edge of the track header to make that track the "star" from which the groove will be applied to other tracks.

You now see a gold star in front of the SoCal track. Also, the checkboxes next to all the other tracks are selected, indicating they will be matching the groove of the SoCal track. I'll refer to these as the "match groove" checkboxes.

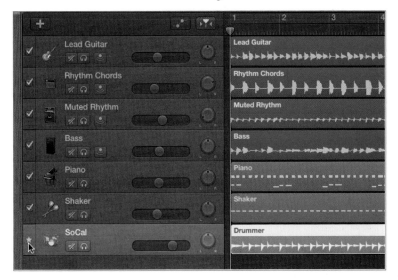

NOTE ▸ You can deselect the match groove checkbox in front of any track to play it without applying groove matching. This may be necessary for vocal performances or instrument parts such as chimes that are intended to come in at a specific time regardless of the rhythm tracks.

7   Play the project to hear the tracks with groove matching applied.

Can you hear the difference? The tracks now sound like musicians jamming together and having a good time.

8   Press C to enter Cycle mode. Play the project and experiment during playback with selecting and deselecting the match groove checkboxes on different tracks. Or you can click the star on the SoCal track to turn off groove matching, and then click again to turn it back on. When you are finished, be sure that SoCal is the groove track and the match groove checkboxes on the other tracks are selected. Save your project.

Now that you've seen how powerful a drummer track can be in controlling other tracks, let's take a look at a subtle drummer feature.

Following the Rhythm of Another Track

You have heard drummer tracks in nearly every project in this book so far. By now you probably have figured out that the virtual drummers are very good at what they do—just like live session drummers. Drummer regions vary automatically between sections of a song to play along with the feel and groove of the music. Sometimes you might want the beat to be influenced by a specific instrument track. For example, during the verse of a song you might want the beat to be influenced by the rhythm guitar, but in the chorus and bridge you want the beat to follow a bass track. Since the Drummer virtual session player is region based, you can edit the drummer beat for each section of the song. In the following exercise you will have Drummer follow a bass track.

1   Open the project **7-2 Drummer Follow** and save it to the My GarageBand Projects folder on the desktop.

The project opens with four tracks: the SoCal Kit drummer track, the Rhythm Guitar L (left) and Rhythm Guitar R (right) tracks, and a bass track.

2   Select the drummer region if it is not already selected. As you can see in the Drummer Editor, Kyle will be the virtual drummer for this demonstration.

3   Play the project once.

Take a careful look at the waveform patterns of the guitar and bass tracks. The notes are all played on the same beat. Also there are noticeable rests, or pauses, between notes.

Now look at the waveform in the drummer track. The waveform shows a consistent drum pattern over both the played notes and the pauses of the other instrument tracks.

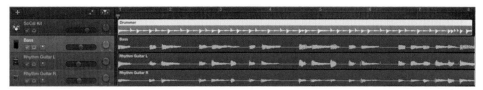

4   In the Drummer Editor, select the Follow Rhythm checkbox (labeled "Follow"). The follow behavior affects the kick and snare portion of the beat, so the slider changes to the Follow Track pop-up menu. For this exercise, the bass track has been selected.

5   Play the project to hear the drum beat follow the bass track. Don't worry if you can't hear the difference (it is subtle unless you are a drummer or have a knack for listening to the kick and snare parts of a drum beat). While watching the drum region, deselect the Follow Rhythm checkbox to see the pattern change, and then select the checkbox again.

Drummer region

Drummer region with follow behavior

NOTE ▶ The follow behavior works best with audio files that are recorded without distortion, overdrive, compressor, or modulation effects using monophonic, polyphonic, or percussive instruments. Also, the notes should be played on the same beat with no overlapping chords.

6   In the Presets list, select a different preset to hear how the kick and snare from that preset beat follow the bass part. Feel free to try as many presets as you like. To me, the

follow behavior is most evident in the presets Half-pipe, Ocean Boulevard, and Paper Hearts. When you are finished, save your project.

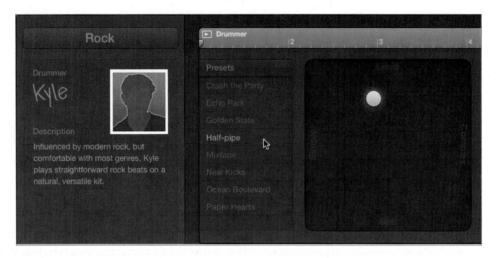

NOTE ▸ When using an audio track, make sure the Enable Flex checkbox for the track is selected in the Audio Editor.

In the previous exercise, you worked with groove matching, which is designed to salvage tracks by fixing the timing. What you just witnessed in this exercise is one of the little finessing details a music producer would use to add professional polish to a song.

Recording Multipass Drum Beats

In Lesson 4, "Recording and Editing Software Instruments," you recorded both single-take and multitake Software Instrument tracks. In this exercise, you'll explore overdub recording as you record two different drum beats using a drum kit and a MIDI drum machine sound. With overdub recording, you can record into the same region over and over, adding different sounds with each pass in a cycle area.

This method of recording is also referred to as multipass recording. Your goal in the next series of exercises is to record a drum region that combines different drum sounds to create an original "beat." Then you'll create a second multipass region using the arpeggiator. Once you have recorded both drum regions, you'll turn them into loops and add them to the Loop Library.

1   Open the project **7-3 Recording Beats** and save it to the My GarageBand Projects folder on your desktop. The project opens with Cycle mode on and the Library displayed.

2   Press Command-K to show the Musical Typing window.

3   Select the SoCal Cowbell track if it is not already selected. Play the project. Watch the Musical Typing keyboard as the SoCal Cowbell region plays. The Y key lights up each time the cowbell sound is played. Pause playback.

This region is a simple, single-take recording of a cowbell part. The region is two measures (bars) in length and was recorded using the Musical Typing keyboard and the Y key. You've heard my recording of the beat-busting analog superhero of the 70s, the cowbell. Now it's your turn to play it.

4   Press the Y key on your computer keyboard, or click the Y key in the Musical Typing window to play the cowbell sound.

Perfect! You've successfully demonstrated the percussive potential of an ancient bovine tracking device. Clearly, you have just the drum skills needed to record an overdub recording with multiple drum sounds.

5   Mute the SoCal Cowbell track.

In a few minutes, you'll turn the pre-recorded cowbell region—and some regions of your own—into loops and add them to the Loop Library For now I just wanted you to see an example of a simple single-take drum part and boost your confidence in playing a percussion instrument on your computer keyboard.

Setting Preferences for Overdub Software Instrument Recording

Since the advent of recording, there has been dubbing. Dubbing simply means recording "on top of" a previously recorded section. In GarageBand, overdubbing is simply the process of recording a performance on top of another existing performance, thus merging them together into a single region.

If you recall, when you recorded multitake Software Instrument regions in Lesson 4, you first needed to deselect the Cycle Recording checkbox in GarageBand's General preferences. Both multitake and multipass (overdub) recordings use a cycle area to determine the length of a recording. It is the Cycle Recording checkbox that specifies whether a Software Instrument performance using a cycle area is going to be a multitake or an overdub recording.

1   Choose GarageBand > Preferences.

2   In General preferences, select the Cycle Recording checkbox.

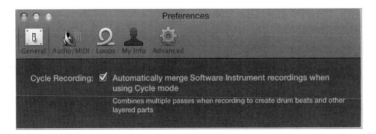

Excellent. Now let's make sure the cycle area is the correct length for your overdub recording and you're good to go.

Recording a Rough Draft

Brace yourself—the first time you try an overdub, Software Instrument recording will likely be rough. Don't worry; with the Undo command, you can always start over. Remember, the Musical Typing window is connected to the selected track.

1   Select the empty SoCal Kit track header at the top of the tracks area. This is the track where you will record your first overdub region.

2   In the Musical Typing window, click the Y key. It should still trigger the MIDI cowbell sound.

Each key on a MIDI keyboard represents a different sound in the SoCal drum kit. You can change octaves using the Z and X keys to play different sounds for the same instrument.

3   Press the Z key on your computer, or click the Z in the Musical Typing window to lower the octave range from C2 to C1.

4   Press or click A to hear the Kick drum (MIDI note C1). Press or click S to hear the snare (MIDI note D1).

5   Start playback. Make sure Cycle mode is turned on and that the cycle area extends from the beginning of bar 1 to the beginning of bar 3. Practice playing the following pattern: (A) kick, (S) snare, (A) kick (A) kick, (S) snare. Repeat that pattern to the click track. Try to play it to the click track and get through the entire pattern in one measure. Then repeat the pattern again for the second measure.

Before recording, experiment with some of the other kit sounds available in the C1 octave range. Once you successfully record your kick and snare pattern, you'll add a few more sounds. Take a moment to come up with two more sounds that you can add to the kick and snare. If you aren't sure what to try, the E key has a nice clap sound, and the black keys T, Y, U, O, and P are all cymbal variations that make a good accent to the kick and snare. Remember, this is just a recording exercise, so whatever you come up with is fine.

For the first pass, you will play only the kick and snare pattern. Choose a second drum sound, pattern, or part for the next pass. Each time you finish recording a drum part, switch to a different sampled drum sound (a different key on the keyboard) to add a new part.

Keep in mind that your drum pattern will be two measures in length, making it a total of eight beats, four per measure.

NOTE ▶ If you are struggling to play the kick and snare together in a pattern, break it up into two separate passes when you record. Try playing the kick drum "A" once on the first beat and twice on the third beat. Repeat for the second measure. Then switch to the snare for the second pass and play "S" once on the second beat, and again on the fourth beat for both measures.

Let's try recording.

6   Press R or click the Record button to start the overdub recording. Let the cycle area play through once and listen to the metronome click track to get a feel for the tempo.

Count to get your timing ready, and then start playing your beat. Keep the recording going until you have recorded a pass with at least four different drum sounds.

The region turns green at the end of a pass and red whenever you are actively play-ing (recording) an instrument part. You can take as many passes as you need between recording parts. The key (pun intended) to making this work is that you *can't* stop recording until you've added all the parts. If you stop recording, the overdub option is over. If you try to record in that region again, you'll erase the previous recording.

7 When you finish, press the Spacebar to stop recording.

8 Play your region to hear how it turned out. If you like everything but the last pass, you can press Command-Z to undo the last pass. Press Command-Z again to delete another pass. If you want to toss the recording and try again, select the region you just recorded and press the Delete key. Click Record and create a new overdub recording.

9 When you are finished, save your project.

You've successfully created a single MIDI region that contains the merged performances from each cycle pass. So, how did it go? Recording drum loops takes a lot of practice and patience. If your region is close except for the timing, you can fix that in the Piano Roll Editor before turning it into a loop.

If you had a rough time creating your overdub MIDI drum kit recording, there's good news. GarageBand includes dozens of pre-recorded drum loops from which to choose. For those of you who like creating your own beats, you now have the tools to do it.

Recording Arpeggiated Drum Machine Beats

For your next attempt at recording an overdub beat, you'll use the Boutique 808 drum machine Software Instrument. With the combination of the Smart Controls and the arpeggiator you'll be able to create great-sounding complex beats with little effort on your part. The best thing about working with drum machine Software Instruments and the arpeggiator is that everything you play should sound pretty good merged into one multipass region.

1   Hide the Library. Press B to show the Smart Controls pane. Mute the SoCal Kit track. Move the Musical Typing window to the top right of the tracks area, where it is out of the way of the track headers, cycle area, and Smart Controls pane.

2   Mute the SoCal Kit track. Select Track 2, which is the first Boutique 808 GB track.

3   Press or click any of the Musical Typing keys to hear the Boutique 808 kit sound for that key.

Since the arpeggiator is turned on, each key triggers a pattern based on the arpeggiator setting and the Mix controls in the Smart Controls area. Take a moment to click all of the black and white keys to hear each of the sounds available in the C1 octave keys for the Boutique 808 drum machine.

You can adjust the level of each kit instrument in the mix by raising or lowering that sound in the Mix controls.

4   Press and hold the O key. You should hear a synth bass along with a pronounced cymbal. While you listen to the O key's sound, click and drag down on the Cymbal knob in the Mix controls to turn down the amount of cymbal sound in the mix. The 10:00 position on the Cymbal dial should leave in enough cymbal to be audible, without the distraction.

5   Press and hold the G key. This time it is the cowbell that is a bit too strong in the mix. In the Smart Controls pane, drag down on the Cowbell knob to lower it to your own taste.

6   Continue playing and adjusting the mix for different keys (sound patterns) on the Musical Typing keyboard. You will use these sounds to record an overdub drum region.

7   Make sure Cycle mode is on and that the cycle region is between bar 1 and bar 3. Practice playing your drum machine pattern; with each pass, you'll add a new arpeggiated note. You can hold the note for the entire recording, or play it several times—it's your party.

8   Press R or click the Record button to begin recording. When you are finished with all four passes or parts (whichever comes first), press the Spacebar to stop.

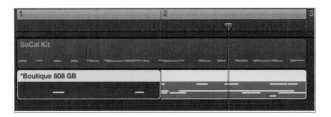

I'm guessing it was much easier to record the arpeggiator-induced beat than the one you had to play manually.

9   Play your newly recorded region. Save your project.

Excellent. Next you'll learn how to turn your own recordings into loops and add them to the Loop Library.

Project Practice

If you'd like to create another overdub drum beat recording, this is your chance. Just mute the first Boutique 808 GB track and select the next track with the same name directly below the one you just recorded in. This time, to make things more interesting choose a different preset from the Arpeggiator pop-up menu. Just remember a track can have only one arpeggiator preset from the menu. If you would like to try a single-take cowbell recording, select the empty SoCal Kit track below the SoCal Cowbell track. Practice with the metronome and the cycle region until you are ready; then turn off Cycle mode and record a take. Or, if you prefer, you could use that same SoCal Kit track to record a multipass (overdub) region using the drum kit instead of the drum machine Software Instrument sound. Have fun. When you are finished, be sure to save your work.

Preparing the Project

Before you start the next series of exercises, let's do a little housekeeping to get the project ready. Also, this is a good time to get a feel for the layout of the regions in the other tracks and why they are arranged the way they are.

1   Close the Musical Typing window and hide the Smart Controls pane.

2   Turn Cycle mode off. Turn off the metronome. Then adjust the horizontal zoom in the timeline until you can clearly see all the regions. There are no regions beyond bar 5.

3   Solo the RSD Stomp Claps track in the middle of the tracks area.

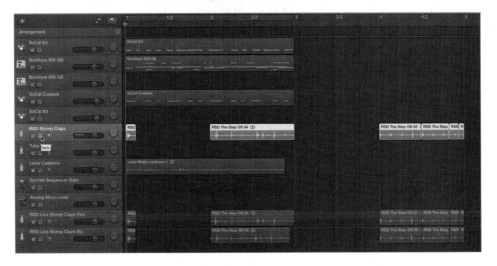

This track includes six audio regions taken from a digital video clip of an award-winning hip-hop dance duet. You'll get to work with the actual video clip and audio track in the next lesson; for now, you'll just create loops from a few snippets of the audio track.

4   Play the project to hear the different regions. Each has musical potential with a little cleanup.

The paired regions in the bottom two tracks are before-and-after versions of the stomps and claps regions that you will be editing shortly. You can use them as a guide if needed. The Lexie Cadence track is an audio recording of my dog walking through leaves.

5   Unsolo the RSD Stomp Claps track and solo the SoCal Cowbell track.

You have now prepared the project and are familiar with the project contents.

Making Recorded MIDI Regions Loop Ready

You can loop any region by dragging the top-right corner of the region in the timeline. Did you know that you can also add your own regions to the Loop Library? Well, you can. However, to create a loop that can be used to build music you'll need to do a few things first. The number one rule for making a region loop-ready is timing. The region must start and end precisely on a measure or beat within a measure (it's best to work with whole measures). Otherwise, as you loop it over and over it will fall out of time with the other parts. Also, the music or percussion part within the region must be in musical time. Sound effects and other nonmusical regions that aren't intended to be repeated as musical parts are referred to as one-shots.

In the next series of exercises, you will make minor adjustments to the regions in this project to prepare a variety of regions ranging from your own drum beat region to a recording of dancers stomping and clapping their own hip-hop beat. Along the way, you'll learn a few new tricks for editing music.

How do you know when a region is loop-ready? One test is to see how it sounds in Cycle mode. Let's start with the SoCal Cowbell.

> **NOTE** ▶ If you did not complete the overdub recording and the previous project exercises, open the project **7-4 Beats for Loops** and save it to your projects folder on the desktop. This project contains beats I recorded while following along with the previous exercises.

1   Turn on Cycle mode and play the project. The SoCal Cowbell region repeats. It sounds like a loop. This region passes test number 1.

The second test is to see if the notes within the region start on beats or ticks in the ruler. You can zoom in and use the grid in the tracks area to determine that.

2   Press Command-Right Arrow to zoom in to the timeline as needed until the ruler shows a decimal point for each beat of the first two measures. Within each beat you will see four tick marks. The grid in the timeline matches the zoom level, so there is a grid line for each tick mark.

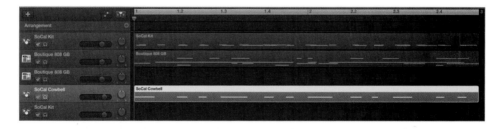

3   Take a look at the SoCal Cowbell region. Do each of the notes within the region start at a grid line? If so, it passes test number 2.

Hint: It will pass, because I used the Time Quantize feature in the Piano Roll Editor to fix the timing right after I recorded it.

Now let's test one of the multipass drum recordings in the top two tracks. Keep in mind that your recordings may not match the examples shown in this book.

4   Unsolo the SoCal Cowbell track. Solo SoCal Kit track (track 1). Play the track. Does it sound like a loop when repeated? Do the notes align with the grid? Chances are they aren't in perfect time—yet.

5   Double-click the region in the SoCal Kit track to open it in the Piano Roll Editor. Adjust the horizontal zoom in the editor so you can clearly see the entire region and all beats as well as ticks between beats.

Each measure is four beats, with four ticks per beat—4 × 4 = 16. So you'll quantize the timing to the nearest 16th note.

6   Choose 1/16 Note from the Quantize pop-up menu. Instantly all of the notes snap to the nearest gridline. That was easy.

7   Play the track to hear the fixed timing. It should sound much better and is now loop-ready.

8   Unsolo the SoCal Kit track and solo the Boutique 808 GB track. The track may already be in perfect time. If not, set the Time Quantize pop-up menu to 1/16 Note. Stop playback and save your project.

The MIDI regions are loop-ready. It's time to work on the audio regions.

Making Recorded Audio Regions Loop-Ready

The added challenge in this exercise is that none of the audio recordings you are going to make into musical loops came from musical instruments. There was no click track other than the actual heartbeats of the performers, and since you can't hear their heartbeats— and neither could they—it doesn't count.

The first region is going to be a one-shot sound effect, so you don't have to worry about timing—you just have to clean up the end with the Trim tool. The second region is a well-executed percussion pattern, but it isn't in perfect musical time. That can be fixed with Flex Time. The third set of regions you will first merge into one region. Then you'll use Flex Time to tweak the timing. Let's get started.

1   Unsolo the Boutique 808 GB track. Select and solo the RSD Stomp Claps track. Turn off Cycle mode.

Adjust the horizontal zoom in the Audio Editor until you can clearly see the first region in the RSD Stomp Claps track.

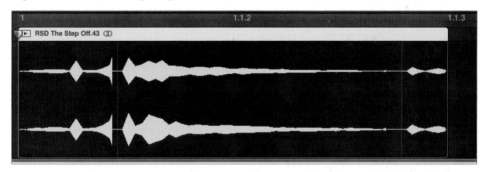

2   Play the region. You can clearly hear a double clap (two people clapping together) and a partial stomp at the end.

Your goal is to trim the right edge to remove the partial stomp after the clap. Fortunately the audio waveform in the Audio Editor shows you exactly where the clap ends and the stomp begins. There is even a convenient silent section (flat line with no waveform) just before the stomp. How did we get so lucky to have such a perfect waveform to work with? Flex Time is turned on.

3   Deselect the purple Flex Time button in the upper left of the editor to hide Flex Time from the waveform in the Audio Editor. The waveform reverts to the original recorded waveform; it's still editable but determining exactly where to trim is not as easy. Click the Flex Time button again to turn it back on.

NOTE ▶ Normally, for sound effects and nonmusical audio regions you wouldn't use Flex Time. However, since it is applied to a track—all or nothing—we will leave it on to use with the other regions in the track that really need it.

4   In the Audio Editor, drag the right edge of the region toward the left to trim off the stomp portion of the waveform. Flex Time added a convenient vertical line for musical timing purposes, which you can use as a guide to see where to trim.

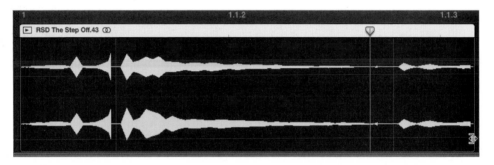

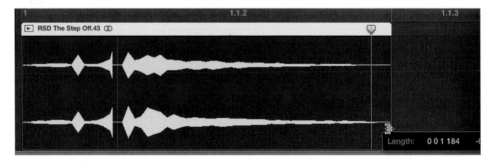

5   Play the trimmed region to hear it. If you only hear the clap without the stomp, mission accomplished. If you still hear stomp, trim more from the right edge.

6   Select the second region in the RSD Stomp Claps track. Adjust the zoom level as needed to focus the visible area in the Audio Editor on the second region.

NOTE ▶ At this zoom level, the ruler in the editor will display the bar (measure), beat (there are four beats per measure), and division of beat (divided into quarters 1–4). So if the ruler in the editor shows 2.3.3, you are looking at bar 2, beat 3, third quarter of the beat.

7   Turn on Cycle mode and create a cycle area from bar 2 to bar 3. You can drag the top part of the ruler in the timeline or in the ruler in the Audio Editor to create the cycle area.

8   Play the cycle area to hear whether the region sounds like a percussion loop.

It actually sounds pretty good on its own. But if you look carefully, you'll see that most of the visible claps and stomps in the waveform do not match up with the grid lines. This means if you tried to use this region as a loop in a musical piece, it would always be slightly out of time with everything else. Another thing to note is that the region isn't exactly one measure in length. Part of the region is beyond the cycle area. Remember the first rule of loop-making is regions have to be the right length.

9   Trim the right edge of the region until it ends exactly at bar 3. The trim overlay will show a new length of exactly one measure (1 0 0 0).

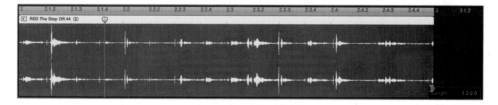

Don't worry about the little bit of stomp sound remaining at the end of the loop. If you listen to playback it actually works, with the stomp at the beginning of the region making it loop seamlessly. The real issue for this region is the timing.

Working with Flex Markers in the Audio Editor

Quantizing and groove tracks work wonders on entire tracks or regions. However, occasionally you may have individual notes that need manual tweaking. For a Software Instrument region, that's easily done with the Time Quantize feature in the Piano Roll Editor, but how do you manipulate notes in an audio region? Once again, the answer lies in the Audio Editor. Flex Time technology analyzes every note, including audio waveforms. Seeing (or hearing) is believing, so let's venture into the editor to adjust the timing of the stomps and claps in the audio region so they will hit right on a beat or beat division mark on the ruler or in the grid.

1   In the Audio Editor, toggle the Flex Time button off, then on again, while looking at the selected region in the editor. You'll see that when Flex Time is showing, the region darkens and the waveform brightens to make it easier to see. Also, the grid lines show up nicely for easier alignment.

NOTE ▶ Be careful where you drag in the Audio Editor. Clicking or dragging the waveform can select, move, or change Flex Time depending where you click. If you accidentally move or change something, press Command-Z to undo the error.

2   Move the pointer slowly across the waveform without clicking. If you look carefully, you'll see the pointer has turned into a Flex pointer that looks like three bars most of the time but changes from three bars to what looks like three playheads whenever you pass over a *transient* (a peak in the waveform).

Clicking on the waveform at or near transients will create a flex marker. The cool thing about flex markers is that you can drag them to the nearest beat or tick in the ruler to fix the timing of that note (or in this case, clap). Flex markers can be moved to manipulate music or to act as barriers so that changes don't ripple down the line and affect earlier notes by mistake.

3   Click the flex pointer just before the first large clap in the waveform at around 2.1.2 in the ruler. Drag the flex marker to the left to the 2.1.2 grid line. The flex markers are attracted to the beats and tick lines in the ruler like magnets, so the marker will snap to the ruler or grid line once you are close enough.

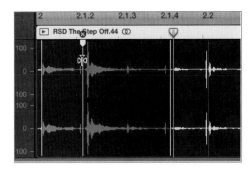
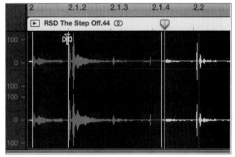

4   Move down the next major peak in the waveform, around 2.2. Click over the waveform peak, and then drag the flex marker left slightly to the 2.2 mark in the ruler.

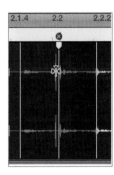
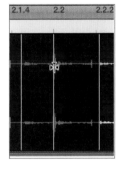

5   Continue working your way down the waveform, fixing the timing of the largest peaks
using flex markers. If the waveform has a thick section with several lower peaks combined, you can align the middle, beginning, or end with the nearest mark in the ruler
depending on how you want it to sound.

Many of your flex edits will be barely noticeable out of context—when you're just listening to the region. But if you plan to add the region to a musical piece as a percussion
loop, the timing is crucial.

6   When you are finished flex editing the region, play the region. Then save your project.

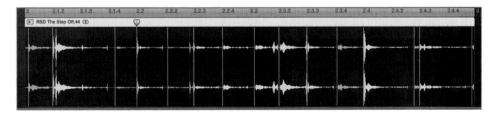

> **NOTE** ▶ Flex markers will be visible only when you hover the flex pointer over it. Stretching or moving a note using flex editing does not change the note's pitch. The more you work with flex editing, the easier it will be to use. Also, to undo a flex edit, click the (x) at the top of the flex marker.

Voilà! Not only did you just complete a bit of waveform timing magic, but you also have a basic understanding of how to use Flex Time to fix individual notes in the Audio Editor.

Now that you have used flex editing to fix the timing of the second stomp and clap region, it's time to work with the last set of regions in the track.

Merging Audio Regions

The next potential loop in the RSD Stomp Claps track consists of a group of four different audio regions that have been edited from the original dance audio track and are arranged together in the timeline. Trouble is, since they are separate regions, you won't be able to add them to the Loop Library as a single loop. Also, it would be easier to edit the timing in the Audio Editor if they were one region. In this exercise you are going to merge the separate regions into one finished region. Technically you don't have to merge them to fix their timing, but doing so ensures that you don't have space between regions. And it is necessary to add them as a single region to the Loop Library. Merging regions is often done with music recordings to create a finished track or section that can then be looped or duplicated more easily as a single region.

1   In the timeline, create a new cycle area from bar 4 to bar 5. It should be exactly one measure in length (1 0 0 0).

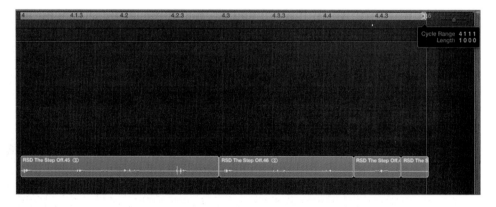

2   Play the cycle area to hear the audio regions together. Click the empty space in the tracks area to deselect all the regions in the RSD Stomp Claps track.

To merge the regions, they need to be together (which they are) and selected.

3   Click the empty space just before the group of clips and drag a marquee around the four RSD The Step Off regions.

Now only the regions you plan to merge are selected in the track.

4   Choose Edit > Join Regions. A dialog appears warning you that noncontiguous audio regions require that you create a new audio file. Click Create.

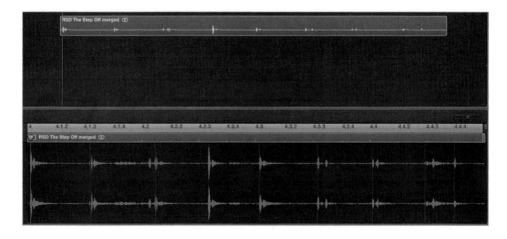

TIP ▶ If you are joining separate audio regions into a merged file, it's a good idea to create a copy of the regions first in case you want to work with them separately at another time. In this project, the copy has already been made in the lower tracks of the timeline.

A new blue audio region called "RSD The Step Off merged" appears in place of the other regions. If you look at the merged region in the Audio Editor, you'll see that the transients (claps and stomps) still need to be aligned with the ruler marks. Also notice the Enable Flex checkbox is selected in the Audio Editor inspector. This option must be selected in order to use Flex Time editing on blue or purple audio regions. The previous regions were orange, which means they were considered imported nonmusical regions, and selecting this checkbox was not necessary.

Take a few minutes to fix the timing of the last region. Then we will add the regions to the Loop Library.

Project Practice

It's your turn to fix the timing of the claps and stomps in the merged audio region. In the Audio Editor you'll see that, at each transient in the waveform, flex processing has already added vertical lines (flex markers) that you can use to drag the transient left to the nearest ruler mark. Now that you've had some practice, this shouldn't take more than a minute. Trim the right and left edges of the merged audio region so that it starts at bar 4 and ends exactly at bar 5. Play the edited region to hear it.

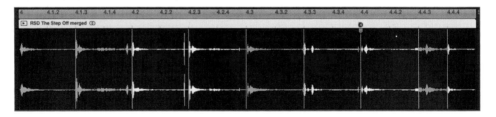

When you are finished, hide the editor and unsolo the RSD Stomp Claps track. Then save your progress.

Adding Regions to the Loop Library

Once you've made a region loop-ready, all you need to do is select the region and choose File > Add Region to Loop Library. Files in the Loop Library will then show up in the loop browser to use in your projects.

In this exercise you'll add seven different regions to the Loop Library, starting with the SoCal Cowbell. Since you already know what the regions sound like, there is no reason to solo the tracks or play them at this time.

1   In the tracks area, select the SoCal Cowbell region. Choose File > Add Region to Loop Library. The Add Region to Apple Loops Library dialog opens.

Here you can name the region, as well as specify whether it is a loop or one-shot. You can also choose instrument descriptors and mood buttons appropriate for your new loop.

2   For this cowbell loop, keep the name as is. Under Instrument Descriptors, choose Percussion > Cowbell. Then select the Single, Clean, and Acoustic mood buttons. When you are finished, click Create.

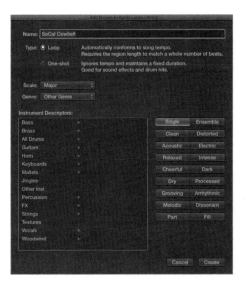 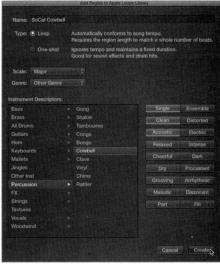

That's all there is to it!

3   Now you can add the remaining regions to the library as follows:

SoCal Kit—Name: *SoCal Beat*; Type: Loop; Instrument Descriptors: All Drums > Beats; mood buttons: Acoustic, Dry, Part

Boutique 808 GB—Name: *Boutique 808 Beat*; Type: Loop; Instrument Descriptors: All Drums > Beats; mood buttons: Electric, Grooving, Part

1st region in RSD Stomp Claps track—Name: *RSD Clap*; Type: One-shot; Instrument Descriptors: FX > People; mood buttons: Single, Clean

2nd region in RSD Stomp Claps track—Name: *RSD The Step Off Beat 01*; Type: Loop; Instrument Descriptors: Other Inst; mood buttons: Clean, Acoustic, Grooving

3rd region in RSD Stomp Claps track—Name: *RSD The Step Off Beat 02*; Type: Loop; Instrument Descriptors: Other Inst; mood buttons: Clean, Acoustic, Grooving

Lexie Walks cadence—Name: *Dog cadence*; Type: One-shot; Instrument Descriptors: Other Inst; mood buttons: Clean, Acoustic

4 Press O to display the loop browser. Click the Loops pop-up menu at the top of the browser and choose My Loops.

Your loops appear in the list at the bottom of the browser. Now you can search for them and use them in projects just like other loops and one-shots.

5 Save your project.

Well done. You have the skills needed to turn any of your recordings or edited audio regions into loops and add them to the Loop Library.

Working with the Tempo Track

In the last exercise, you will explore how the project tempo can be manipulated as part of the song. As promised, you are going to use your newly created loops to enhance a cool hip-hop beat. You've already learned enough about creating and editing drum and percussion tracks to build a solid beat. However, since hip-hop is not a music genre I work with often, I figured it best to consult a professional.

I talked with professional independent hip-hop artist and songwriter Colby Stiltz to get his take on what makes a great hip-hop beat. His advice in a nutshell: "Find the easiest way to modify a sound from its original vibration to a new creation." To him, tempo is a big deal. He likes projects around 80 bpm, but it all depends on the song. It could be 120 bpm and you could half-time the beat and rap half as fast so it's like a slow flow. Or if it's closer to 70 bpm, you could double-time the beat and rap really fast. Every tempo has its place somewhere. In other words, if the beat is slow you can rap twice as fast to mix it up, or if the beat is fast you can rap half the speed. Of course you also have the option to rap at the same speed as the beat, but what's the fun in that?

> **MORE INFO** ▶ For more information about Colby Stiltz and his music, visit his website: http://funwithstiltz.com.

Let's dive into a very basic hip-hop beat in progress and add changes in the tempo to make it more interesting.

1 Open the project **7-5 Beats and Tempo** and save it to your projects folder.

   The project opens with one Software Instrument, Steinway Grand Piano track, and six different beat tracks from various Apple Loops. Notice that Groove Match is showing in the track headers, and the piano part is being controlled by the Blueprint Beat 01 track.

2 Play the first half of the project. Listen for the pause in the piano part around bar 13. This was created deliberately to make room for a dramatic tempo change.

   To add or edit tempo changes within the project, you need to use Tempo track.

3 Choose Track > Show Tempo Track. The Tempo track appears at the top of the timeline just below the ruler.

The project is currently set to Colby's favorite hip-hop tempo, 80 bpm. In the tempo track, tempo changes are represented by control points on the tempo curve. Believe it or not, the straight line in the tempo track is called the tempo curve. Each parameter that can be automated is represented by a curve (line) that can be bent or curved using control points. At the moment there are only two tempo control points—one at the beginning of the track (bar 1) and one at the end of the track. To add tempo control points, you double-click the tempo curve.

NOTE ▶ It's best to keep your playhead parked at the beginning of the project while adding control points to a curve. If you create an extra control point by mistake, or need to delete your control points for any reason, you can draw a marquee around them and delete at any time.

4   Adjust the horizontal zoom in the timeline as needed until you can see a number in the ruler for each measure (bar). Double-click the tempo curve at bar 13 to add a control point at that position. Double-click the tempo curve at bar 22 to add another tempo control point.

5   Click the tempo curve (straight line) between the two tempo control points that you just added to select that section of the curve. Drag the selected curve between your control points upward to a tempo of 120 bpm.

The tempo curve for the project now clearly shows a tempo of 80 bpm at the beginning and end of the song, with a section at 120 bpm in the middle.

6   Play the middle of the project to hear the tempo change and see how it affects both the beats and the piano part.

Works great. Now let's add one more set of control points. This time you'll make the transition from one tempo to the next more gradual (curved).

7   Double-click the tempo curve at bar 26 to add a control point. Move to bar 28 and Control-Option-Command-click the curve. A field appears to enter the new tempo value. Type 65 in the field and press Return.

The new control point appears and is in position at 65 bpm at bar 28. To curve the transition between the control points, you can drag the upper control point at bar 28 to turn it into a handle that bends the curve.

8   Click the upper control point at bar 28 to turn it into a curve handle. Drag the handle up and to the left to make it a more gradual curve.

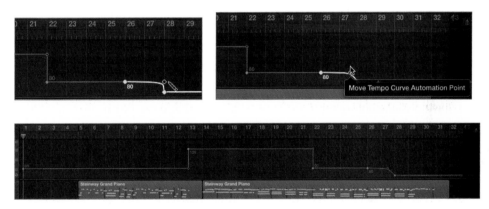

9   Play the project to hear the dramatic tempo changes in the music. Save your progress.

Clearly, tempo changes can be a powerful tool in making a musical piece more dramatic.

Project Tasks

Time to fix up and mix up this hip-hop beat to make it more interesting. The tempo changes are already in place. In the loop browser, grab the loops you created and add them to the project. Feel free to delete any of the current loops in the project and replace them with some of your own selections from the browser. If you want to try several different versions of this project, just save the project with a different name and try again. When you are finished, save your project.

If you want to see and hear the crazy beat I made using all the loops we created earlier, plus a few other odds and ends, open the project **7-6 MP Crazy Beat**.

In this project, you'll notice that all of the tracks have green locks in the track headers. This project includes a lot of heavy processing effects. Locking tracks protects them from accidental change by "freezing" the tracks and creating files with the effects already rendered.

Lesson Review

1. What methods are available in GarageBand for fixing timing issues in recorded regions?
2. How do you change the beat in a drummer region so that it is influenced by a specific instrument track?
3. Which GarageBand checkbox must be selected for overdub recording with Software Instruments?
4. What are the two most important criteria a region must have to be a good musical loop (loop-ready)?
5. How do you add a region to the Loop Library so that it can be accessed in the loop browser?

Answers

1. GarageBand includes quantizing, groove tracks, and Flex Time editing for fixing timing of regions or individual notes.

2. Select the Follow checkbox in the Drummer Editor, and then choose a track from the Follow Track pop-up menu.

3. The Cycle Recording checkbox in GarageBand General Preferences must be selected for Software Instrument multipass (overdub) recording.

4. Regions must be trimmed so they start and end exactly at the beginning of a measure or beat within that measure. Also, the timing of the performance within the region needs to be in musical time aligned with beats, or divisions of beats.

5. Select the region and choose File > Add Region to Loop Library.

8

Lesson Files

APTS GarageBand Book Files > Lesson 8 > 8-1 Rough Mix, 8-2 Finished Mix, 8-3 EQ Effect Starting, 8-4 EQ Effect Finished

APTS GarageBand Book Files > Lesson Bonus Projects > 8 RSD Bounced Loops, 8 RSD With Loops

APTS GarageBand Book Files > Additional Media > RSD The Step Off.m4v

Time

This lesson takes approximately 30 minutes to complete.

Goals

Evaluate a rough music mix

Pan guitar tracks and add EQ effect presets

Work with the master track presets

Automate volume and pan curves in a track

Reconnect a movie file to a project

Enhance the audio track of a movie clip

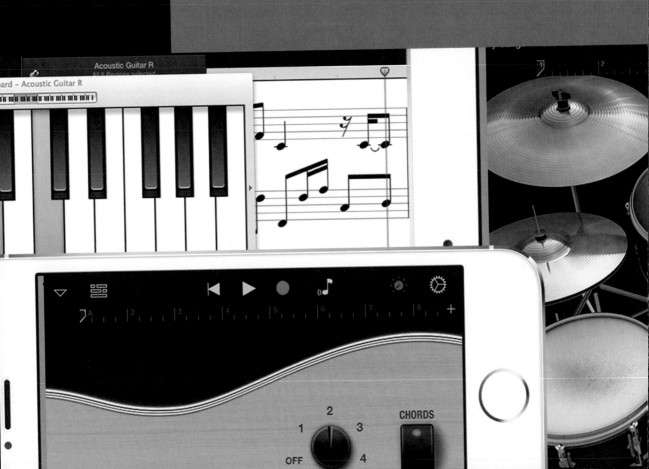

Mixing Music and Adding EQ Effects

With GarageBand, you can record and create professional-quality music. However, to make your finished songs actually *sound* professional, you need to understand the fine art of mixing music.

Fortunately, the GarageBand interface includes an easy-to-use track mixer with controls for volume level and pan position. There is also a full complement of automation curves that you can use to create changes over the course of a song. They can be used to highlight certain tracks at a specific time, have a track pan back and forth between the left and right sides of the stereo field to create acoustic movement between speakers, or modify the amount of an effect applied to a track at a particular time.

If you have been following along with the lessons in this book, you have already worked with the volume levels in individual tracks, and you have even panned tracks. You have also gained quite a bit of hands-on experience adding effects to tracks, changing presets and patches, and even modifying the effects in the Smart Controls pane.

In this lesson you will focus on some advanced mixing techniques, starting with the EQ (equalizer) effect. This powerful new GarageBand tool allows you to dramatically optimize the sound of a track or the entire song. You'll also work with the volume and pan automation curves, as well as explore the master track to add effects to the overall project.

Your goal in this lesson is to use the EQ effect to improve the sound of a video clip. Then you'll take an arranged song to the next level to make it sound like a professional composition. To accomplish this, you'll need to apply professional mixing techniques, including balancing volume, panning tracks, and adding automation to the volume and pan curves to finesse the mix. Along the way, you'll also learn some handy shortcuts and mixing tricks.

Evaluating a Rough Music Mix

If you have been following the lessons in this book, you have already worked with the Volume sliders and Pan knobs in the track headers. In this project, the volume levels already have been adjusted, just as you would while arranging the song. Once you finish arranging tracks, it is time to evaluate your mix.

You need to listen for three things:

▶   Are the volume levels of the different instrument tracks blended (mixed) so that they work together?

▶   Do any of the instrument parts stand out as being too loud or too quiet?

▶   Do you hear instrument parts spread out in the stereo field between the left and right headphones/speakers?

In this exercise you'll open the project and play it to evaluate the rough mix and fix any tracks that are too loud or quiet. Also, you'll adjust the pan dials to separate some of the instruments in the panoramic stereo field.

1   Open the project **8-1 Rough Mix**. Then save the project in your My GarageBand Projects folder on the desktop.

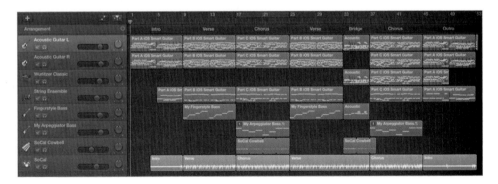

2   Play the project to evaluate the rough mix.

Could you hear that all the tracks are panned to the center—meaning the volume is the same out of both speakers? What did you think of the SoCal Cowbell loop that was added to the chorus and bridge sections of the song? It's hard to miss because the volume level of the cowbell loop is overpowering. Let's start by turning down the volume of the SoCal Cowbell track. After all, sometimes you don't want more cowbell.

3   Turn on Cycle mode. There should be a cycle area over the chorus section of the song. Start playback. While listening to the cowbell part in the mix, drag the Volume slider on the SoCal track to lower its volume level until it sounds more like an accent to the drumbeat. When you are finished, stop playback and turn off Cycle mode.

I set my SoCal Cowbell to –8db. Feel free to set yours to whatever level you like. Other than that, there are a few high-pitched notes in the bridge section that I haven't decided whether or not I like. I'll decide after we add some automation and EQ to the master track. The nice thing about MIDI software instrument regions is you can edit them any time.

Next, let's spread out some of the instrument parts in the stereo field.

Panning Tracks

Not only is it important to adjust the volume of a track, but you also need to consider the position in the stereo field where the track is perceived in the listener's ear.

The Pan knob controls the left-to-right placement of a track within the stereo field. The *pan* in Pan knob stands for *panoramic*. A panoramic photograph is an image that includes everything you can see without turning your head. A panoramic stereo field is everything you can hear from the far left to the far right, without turning your head.

By default, all the tracks in GarageBand start with the pan position set to the center (0). When at center pan position, a sound is heard equally out of both speakers as though it's directly in front of you in the middle of the audio space.

In this exercise you'll pan the two guitar tracks to separate them left and right.

1   Solo the top two tracks. Play the soloed tracks to hear them in the stereo field. At the moment you can hear the tracks equally out of both speakers (or headphones). So they sound as though they are coming from the exact same acoustic space in the stereo field. Continue playback while you adjust the Pan knobs for the tracks.

2   In the Acoustic Guitar L track header, click the Pan knob and drag down slowly until the Pan overlay says –40 (40 left). Drag up slowly on the Acoustic Guitar R Pan knob until it says +40 (40 right).

You probably could hear the perceived position of the guitar tracks move left and then right as you adjusted the Pan knobs. However, since both guitar tracks have identical regions and instrument patches, it's hard to hear the separation between parts. To make the tracks sound like two different guitars in different acoustic placement, you need to change the sound of one of them. This is a perfect job for an EQ effect preset.

Working with EQ Effect Presets

Throughout this book you have had quite a bit of hands-on experience with instrument patches, effects, and the Smart Controls pane. One effect you haven't tried yet is the EQ effect.

GarageBand's all new EQ (equalizer) effect is incredibly useful for optimizing the sound of your tracks and projects. It includes eight independent EQ bands arranged from low (bass) to high (treble), presets created for different uses and instruments, and the Analyzer, which shows the frequencies of the track as it plays to help you decide which ones to boost or cut.

You'll find the EQ controls in the Smart Controls pane. In this exercise you'll add a different EQ effect preset to each of the guitar tracks.

1   Unsolo the Acoustic Guitar R track. Select the Acoustic Guitar L track header if needed and make sure it is still soloed.

2   Press B to show the Smart Controls pane. Click the EQ button in the middle of the Smart Controls menu bar to open the Graphic EQ display.

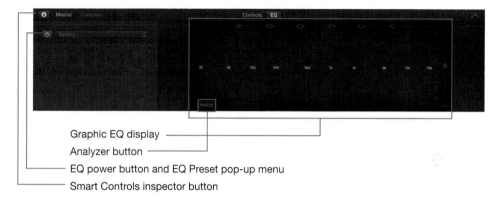

Graphic EQ display
Analyzer button
EQ power button and EQ Preset pop-up menu
Smart Controls inspector button

3   Start playback from the beginning of the song. In the Smart Controls inspector (the left side of the Smart Controls pane), click the EQ Preset pop-up menu and choose Guitar > Acoustic Guitar.

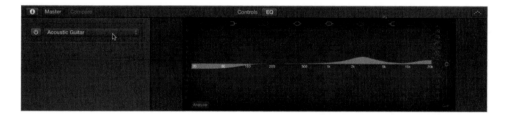

The light blue area in the Graphic EQ display shows which frequencies were raised (over the center line) and which were lowered (below the center line) to create the Acoustic Guitar EQ preset. Can you hear the difference in the sound?

You can definitely hear that the track is panned to the left when it is soloed.

4   Click the EQ power button on and off during playback to hear the Acoustic Guitar L track with and without the EQ. You should be able to hear a slight improvement in the sound with the EQ. Unsolo the Acoustic Guitar L track and solo the Acoustic Guitar R track.

5   Select the Acoustic Guitar R track. Start playback from the beginning of the song. In the EQ Preset pop-up menu choose Guitar > Ultra Bright Guitar.

The Graphic EQ display updates accordingly. You can clearly see and hear a difference. The lower frequencies have been lowered considerably, whereas the higher frequencies are raised to create the "bright" sound.

6   Unsolo both of the guitar tracks and listen to them in the mix (with the other tracks).

The mix sounds really good. Now that the volume levels are balanced, the tracks are panned as needed, and you've added some EQ effects to the guitar tracks, let's add a little EQ to the entire project.

Adding an Effects Patch and EQ to the Master Track

So far, you have worked only with individual instrument tracks in the tracks area. In this section you'll learn about the *master track*, which represents the output for the entire project. Adding an EQ effect to the master track enhances the combined (mixed) output of all the tracks. Let's try it.

1   Choose Track > Show Master Track. The master track appears as the lowest track in the timeline. Double-click the master track header to see the master effects patches available in the Library.

The master effects patches are combinations of EQ and compressor effects. You can turn the effects on and off, or modify them by clicking the Output button (next to the EQ button) in the Smart Controls menu.

2   Start playback from the beginning of the song. In the Library, select the Top 40 patch for the master track. Click the Output button to see the output controls for the master track.

Hello, Top 40! The difference in the overall sound is incredible. This little ditty almost sounds like a Top 40 hit. (Well, maybe Top 400, but still, what a difference a master effect patch can make on the overall sound.)

3   In the Library, try some of the various master effect patches to compare them. Feel free to toggle back and forth between the Output and EQ displays in the Smart Controls pane to see which effect settings and equalizer frequencies are used to create such dramatically different sounds. When you're finished, select the Top 40 master preset.

4   Hide the Library and the Smart Controls pane. Save your progress.

Excellent! The mix is done. Let's check the output volume level to make sure it is good.

Evaluating the Master Output Level

You should consider four volume controls as you finish your mix: track volume, master track volume, master output volume, and computer output volume. Each volume control adjusts a particular level. The track volume adjusts the level of the individual track, and the computer output volume controls how loudly you hear the sound from your computer in your speakers or headphones. It's important to understand the difference between the overall song volume, which you control through the master track, and the master output volume.

The master track volume and master output volume both control the combined output volume level of the tracks. The difference is that the master track volume can be automated with volume control points on the master track volume curve, whereas the master output volume is the level that goes out of GarageBand to the computer. This output level determines the level your song will have when it is exported or shared—for example, when it is output from GarageBand to iTunes.

Now that you understand the various volume controls, let's look at the master output volume to see whether it needs adjustment.

1 Play the project and watch the master volume meter in the top-right corner of the GarageBand window.

The lower the volume, the shorter the solid-colored bars. If the color is green, the level is within a safe range and isn't too loud. If the color turns from green to yellow, that means caution—your sound is bordering on being too loud. If it turns red, you need to stop and turn down the volume immediately. If you don't, the sound could become distorted.

NOTE ▶ The level meters in GarageBand are *sticky*, which means a single line of the colored bar will stick to the highest position on the meter while the average levels continue to change. The average volume level is indicated by the solid-colored bar, and the peaks are marked with the vertical line.

You should see the meters turn red around the end of the verse and stay there through the chorus and the rest of the song.

2 Play the chorus (the loudest part of the song) and slowly drag the Master Volume slider to the left until the meter shows solid green bars with a bit of solid yellow at the top.

Terrific. The song is ready to share. Unless…you want to add a few mixing tricks to bring out the cowbell part in the mix. Why not?

Working with Volume and Pan Automation Curves

So far, you have adjusted the volume and pan levels for individual tracks by using the controls in the track mixer. This method is great for setting one volume or pan level for an entire track. But what if you want the level to change during the song?

Your goal in this exercise is to use control points to create a fade on the volume curve of the SoCal Cowbell track so that the cowbell sound doesn't end so abruptly. Then you'll add control points to the track's pan curve so the cowbell sound roams back and forth between the left and right speakers during the song.

To make changes to an automation curve, you first need to show the track automation curves in the timeline.

1   Press A (for *automation*), or click the Automation button in the tracks area menu bar. All of the tracks in the timeline expand to accommodate automation curves. Each track header also includes an Enable Automation button and an Automation Parameter pop-up menu. The default setting in the Automation Parameter pop-up is the Volume curve.

2   In the SoCal Cowbell track header, click the Enable Automation button.

A yellow volume automation curve appears above the regions in the track and runs the length of the project.

3   Select the second SoCal Cowbell region in the track. Adjust the horizontal zoom level in the timeline so that you can clearly see the entire selected region in the tracks area.

4   In the SoCal Cowbell track, double-click the volume automation curve (line) at bar 37 to add a control point. (Hint: There is a notch where the loop repeats at that same position.)

5   Add another control point at the end of the region (bar 38). Drag the second control point down to the lowest level.

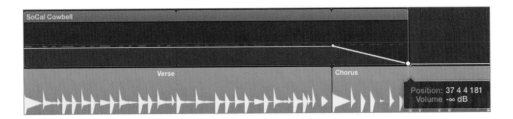

You just created a fade in the volume curve. Now let's automate a panning curve over this same region.

6   In the SoCal Cowbell track, select Pan from the Automation Parameter pop-up menu.

A green pan curve appears in the track. For pan curves, the center of the automation area is panned center (0), above the line it's panned left, and below the line it's panned right. The farthest you can pan left is –64; the farthest right is +63.

7   Add control points to the beginning, middle, and end of the region.

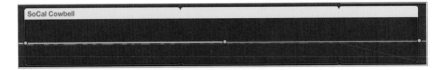

8   Drag the middle control point down to a level of +50 (panned right +50). Drag the first and third control points up to a level of –50 (panned left –50).

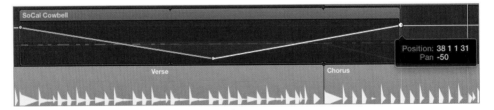

9   Solo the SoCal Cowbell track and play the track from bar 33 to bar 38 to hear the automated panning of the cowbell and the fade-out between bar 37 and 38.

Now let's add panning automation to the first cowbell region.

10 Scroll the tracks area until you clearly see the first SoCal Cowbell region. Add five control points: one at the beginning, one at the end, and one at each notched area where the loop repeats. Raise or lower each control point so that the sound alternates between the left and right speakers. How much you pan each time is up to you.

11 When you are finished, play the region to hear your panoramic automation. Then unsolo the track and listen to the automated cowbell in the mix. When you are finished, press A to hide track automation and save your progress.

If you didn't finish all the exercises in this lesson and want to hear the finished mix, open the project **8-2 Finished Mix**.

NOTE ▶ Hiding track automation does not turn it off. To remove a track control point, you can select and delete the point. To remove all automation from a track, choose Mix > Delete All Automation on Selected Track. To move all the points on a curve the same amount at once, Option-click a point and reposition it while holding down Option.

Congratulations. You've finished mixing the project, and you've added a few advanced tricks with automation and effects to enhance the project. Now you can apply these mixing techniques to your own projects. And your newly trained ear will hear all kinds of mixing and panning automation hidden in your favorite music.

In the next section you'll add an EQ effect to the audio track of a video clip to enhance the sound.

Preparing the Project and Reconnecting a Movie File

The project you are about to open is based on a movie file. So far, the only movie file you've worked with in this book has been the movie of my dog walking that you added to the movie track in Lesson 2. In this lesson you'll open a project that already has a clip in the movie track. There's just one catch: Movie files are not saved in the package contents of a GarageBand project file. So whenever you move a GarageBand project containing a movie from one computer to another, you'll need to reconnect the movie. Luckily, it takes only a few seconds to do so.

1   Open the project **8-3 EQ Effect Starting**. A warning dialog appears to let you know the movie is missing.

If you read the path of the movie file in the dialog, you'll note that it is the same location as the movie file on your computer. So all you need to do is show GarageBand where to find it.

2   Click the Locate File button. When the Locate File dialog opens, navigate to Desktop > APTS GarageBand Book Files > Additional Media Files > RSD The Step Off.m4v.

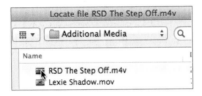

3   Double-click the **RSD The Step Off.m4v** file to open it. Then save the project in your My GarageBand Projects folder on the desktop.

Now that the project is open and the movie file connected, you're ready to add some EQ.

Evaluating the Overall Sound

Although the project you opened does not contain music per se, you can still double tracks and add EQ to the movie's audio track to enhance the overall sound. First, you'll need to play the project and evaluate the audio track that came with the movie. Once you listen to a movie's audio track, you'll have a better idea of what improvements, if any, it needs.

Movie audio tracks always appear in the top track and have the same name as the movie file. In this project, you'll notice there are also three other muted tracks. We'll get to those shortly. In the interest of saving time, and to avoid reteaching things you've already learned, I set up this project like a cooking show with some of the ingredients already prepped and ready to add to the mix (pun intended).

The award-winning dancers in this video are Lauren Diaz and Brooke Bingham, both teen-aged dancers from the Ready Set Dance competition team in Gotha, Florida. The gentleman at the end of the video clip is William Blair, the choreographer for this dance. He specializes in mainstream pop, hip-hop, and music-video dance choreography. When I first saw this *a cappella* (without accompanying instruments or music) portion of Lauren and Brooke's dance, it caught my attention as a powerful example of noninstrumental percussion for this book. Plus, it's a cool dance to watch that lends itself well to audio enhancement—not to mention the potential for making audio loops from the soundtrack, which you already worked with in the previous lesson.

> **MORE INFO ▶** To learn more about the Ready Set Dance classes, staff, and competition team, check out http://readysetdance.com. You also can see more about their performances and awards on Facebook at https://www.facebook.com/ReadySetDanceOrlando.

For now, let's watch and listen to the movie and its audio track. Don't be surprised if the stomps and claps in this hip-hop dance routine sound familiar. Some of the loops you created in the previous lesson came from the RSD The Step Off movie's audio track.

1   In the movie track header, click the minimized movie window to expand it. Feel free to resize the movie window by freely dragging one of its corners.

2   Move the movie window to the empty space at the bottom of the tracks area. Then
play the project.

What do you think? To me, the visual part of the hip-hop dance performance is exciting and captivating. However, the audio of their dramatic stomps and claps is so lackluster it detracts from the overall experience. When the dancers perform in an auditorium on stage, the stomps and claps pack a lot more punch. Since this video was shot at the Ready Set Dance Studio on a cushioned floor designed for tumbling, the acoustic power of this performance has been significantly reduced. Your goal in the next exercise is to use the EQ effect to reshape the sound to make it worthy of the awesome dancers in the video.

Now that we have determined that the sound for this clip should be louder, let's listen to the track doubled to hear if that gives it a boost.

3   Select the Doubled Audio track header. Press M to unmute the track. Play the first part of the project again and listen to it with the doubled audio tracks. As the project plays, toggle the Mute button on and off by pressing the M key to hear it with and without the doubled track. When you are finished, make sure the Mute button is turned off.

Did you hear a difference with the doubled track? It definitely sounded louder with the second track. You may be wondering why I doubled the track instead of just cranking up the track's volume in the track header. A rule of audio mixing is that if you have to drag a volume slider all the way up to properly hear a track, you should find another way to raise it. Why? Because when you add other effects or tracks to the mix, you have nowhere to go. You can only turn the level down—you can't give it a little extra volume later if needed. Audio is cumulative, so adding a track to itself boosts the amplitude (volume) instantly, while giving you room to still raise the level further later.

Clearly, just doubling the track isn't enough. Time to break out the GarageBand EQ effects and bring this soundtrack to life.

Working with the Analyzer and the Graphic EQ

You've already worked with the EQ effect presets earlier in this lesson. What if there isn't a track preset that optimizes the frequencies you need? Since there isn't a preset for *a cappella* hip-hop dance on cushioned floor, you'll have to create your own or modify an existing preset as needed. For this exercise you'll do the latter.

How do you know what frequencies you need to boost or reduce? You use the built-in Analyzer. First you'll solo the track and use the Analyzer to see the frequency curve for the track. Then you'll use the Graphic EQ to boost the frequencies that enhance the stomps and claps.

1   Select the Doubled Audio track, if it is not already selected. Then press B to display the Smart Controls pane and press Y to show the Library. Move and resize the movie window as needed so you can see the Smart Controls pane.

2   In the Smart Controls menu, click the EQ button. If you look at the Library you'll see that the Natural Vocal patch has already been applied to the track.

Let's solo the Doubled Audio track so it will be easier to hear the changes in the EQ as you make them. Also, this is a good time to turn on Cycle mode so that you can continuously hear the dance sounds while you experiment with the EQ.

3   Press S to solo the Doubled Audio track. Press C to turn on Cycle mode. You should see a cycle area from around 5 seconds (0:05) to around 50 seconds (0:50). If for some reason you don't already have one of that length, create it now. The length of the cycle area doesn't need to be precise; it just has to be long enough to cover the majority of the dance.

Now all we have to do is figure out which frequencies need adjusting in the Graphic EQ. Luckily, the Analyzer can show us.

4   Start playback. In the lower-left corner of the Graphic EQ display, click the Analyzer button.

The Analyzer displays the frequency curve for the selected track. The light blue shaded areas in the EQ show the frequency curve applied to the track by the Natural Vocal patch. If you watch the live frequency curve from the Analyzer you'll see that it conforms to the frequency boundaries imposed by the Natural Vocal patch.

The Analyzer shows frequency activity between 100 and 500 Hz every time the girls stomp, and around 5000 Hz (5K) for the claps.

TIP ▶ The Analyzer is processor intensive while the EQ display is visible, so it's important to turn it off when you are finished.

5   In the Graphic EQ display, hover the pointer over the 200 Hz range. The area becomes shaded yellow and a yellow control point appears in the middle.

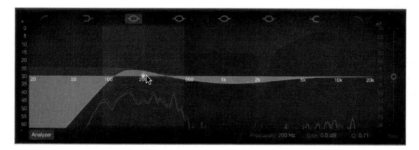

6   Drag the yellow EQ handle (point) down to hear what happens when you remove the 200 Hz frequencies. The stomps are barely audible. Drag the yellow handle up to around 20 on the graph. Drag it left and right between 100 Hz and 500 Hz to hear which range works best for the stomps. Toggle the EQ power button on and off as needed to hear the track with and without the modified EQ.

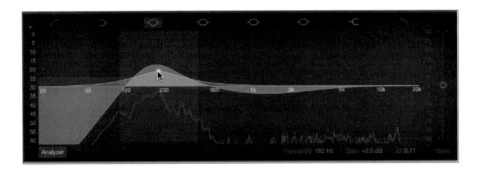

Once you are satisfied with your improvements to the stomps, it's time to fix the claps.

7   Hover between 2k and 5k. The area becomes shaded blue. At the bottom of the EQ display, the exact frequency the handle is set to appears (2500 Hz). Drag the blue handle down to remove the frequency, then up, left, and right until you find what sounds best for the claps. You can see my choice of 3450 Hz in the screenshot.

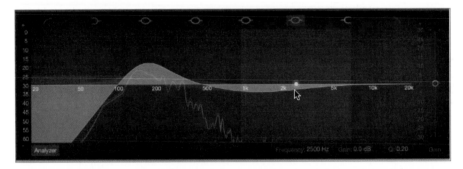

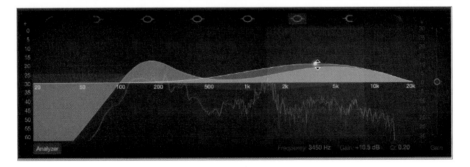

8   Click the Smart Controls inspector button (i) if the inspector is not showing. Toggle
     the EQ power button off and on to hear the difference you've made to the EQ. Feel
     free to experiment with the Graphic EQ before moving on to the next step. If you
     want to reset the EQ, choose Recall Default from the EQ Preset pop-up menu.

     NOTE ▶ The symbols at the top of the Graphic EQ represent the eight independent
     equalizer bands. Each band has its own color and can be turned on or off as needed.
     If you like the frequency curve you created but find it is a bit too loud or quiet, you
     can use the Gain slider on the right edge of the display to lower or raise the level
     without changing your curve.

     Now that you have greatly improved the sound of the performance, let's hear it with
     all the tracks.

9   Press C to turn off Cycle mode. Click the Analyzer button to turn it off. Unsolo the
     Doubled Audio track and unmute the bottom two tracks. Play the end of the perfor-
     mance to hear the last two tracks. See if you can guess what sound was used for the
     region in the Guitar 1 track.

     The guitar track region is actually just the impact sound of Lauren and Brooke's feet
     when they landed after their spectacular backflips at the end of the performance. I copied
     and pasted that part of the region into a guitar track so I could add some echo, reverb,
     and other guitar sound effects. The final track is my daughter saying "Awesome" from
     her Wah Kazoo recording session. I added plenty of electric guitar and amp effects to
     modify her voice.

The final step is to add an EQ effect preset to the master track. You don't even have to display the master track in the timeline.

10 In the Smart Controls inspector, click the Master button. In the Library, choose a Factory preset for the master track. Feel free to experiment with different presets or the Output controls in the Smart Controls. When you are finished, solo the top track to hear the original sound with no effects, then unsolo the track to hear your finished version. If you'd like to hear my finished version of the project, open 8-4 **EQ Effect Finished**.

Mixing audio tracks and adding effects get easier the more you practice. Now you have the mixing and effects skills to greatly improve the sound of your own projects.

Bonus Exercise 1

You have added EQ to the RSD The Step Off project, but what would happen if you added loops as well? To build up the soundtrack even more, you could add the loops you created or something entirely different from the loop browser. Audition a few loops from the browser to see how they sound, and see what you can make fit with the project. Hint: Their dance isn't following any audible music, so you may need to make the loop tracks you add follow the original dance audio track's groove.

Have fun. I've included two examples in the Lesson Bonus Projects folder. The first is called 8 **RSD Bounced Loops**. Open this version if you are working with the 500 original loops that came with GarageBand 10. In this project, I exported the tracks with added loops into one file that I then added to a different version of the project. This process is also called "bouncing" audio. If you have the full set of 2,000 Apple Loops that come with the one-time download, open the project 8 **RSD With Loops** to see and hear the project with the added loops. In each project, you will need to locate the movie clip in the Additional Media folder.

Bonus Exercise 2

If you enjoyed balancing volume between audio tracks, panning, and adding effects, here is your opportunity to try another project. Open the project Loopy Ringtone from your My GarageBand Projects folder, or the version 3-4 **Loopy Ringtone Finished** project in the Lesson 3 folder and save it to your My GarageBand Projects folder. Listen to the project, then create a rough mix by balancing the volume levels between tracks. Pan the tracks as needed to create separation in the stereo field. Add automation control points as you like to the track parameter curves. Add the EQ effect to different tracks, or to the master track. Experiment with the different output effects and overall enjoy the process.

Lesson Review

1. Where do you find the pan and volume controls for a track?
2. How can you apply effects or automation to an entire project?
3. How do you create changes over time to a track's volume level or pan position?
4. Where do you find the EQ effect presets for a track?
5. What does the Analyzer in the Graphic EQ do?

Answers

1. The volume and pan controls for a track are in the track mixer area of the track header.
2. The master track lets you apply effects or automation to an entire project.
3. Enable Automation on the track, select a parameter to automate from the Automation Parameter pop-up menu, and add control points to the track's automation curves.
4. You can choose EQ Effect Presets from the pop-up menu in the Smart Controls inspector.
5. The Analyzer shows the frequency curve in the Graphic EQ display of the selected audio track as it plays.

9

Lesson Files   APTS GarageBand Book Files > Lesson 9 > 9 Dog Walk Ditty, 9 Loopy Ringtone, 9 RSD The Step Off, 9 Scales, 9 Lifes Flower

Time   This lesson takes approximately 30 minutes to complete.

Goals   Set preferences for iTunes

Share a ringtone to iTunes

Export a project as a movie

Fade out the master track

Export a song to disk

Sharing Your Finished Projects

Now that you know the basics of recording, arranging, fixing, and mixing your projects in GarageBand, you're ready to share them to your computer, your iOS devices via iCloud, to a portable disk, to iTunes and the Media Browser so they can be used with other Apple applications like iMovie and Final Cut Pro, or to all of your friends, family, and fans through SoundCloud. In this lesson you'll prepare and share five different projects from this book.

Sharing with Other Apple Applications

If you haven't experienced the ease of working across multiple Apple applications, you will do so shortly as you explore the various ways to share GarageBand projects. The key to integration is the Media Browser, which is accessible from all Apple applications (as well as many other applications).

The Share menu includes six choices that you will explore in the next series of exercises.

When you're ready to share your project, click the Share menu and then choose one of the following commands:

▸ **Song To iTunes**—Place a mixed copy of the track into your iTunes library. You'll explore this option fully in the next section.

▸ **Ringtone to iTunes**—Create a cycle region to determine the ringtone loop, then share the ringtone to iTunes.

▸ **Media Browser**—This command takes the entire project, from the beginning to the end of the last region, and creates an audio file named after the project in the Media Browser. Any silence at the beginning or end of the project is trimmed. If Cycle mode is on, the part within the cycle area is shared to the Media Browser.

▸ **SoundCloud**—If you have a SoundCloud account, you can use this option to share a song to SoundCloud directly from GarageBand.

▸ **Export Song to Disk**—Save an MP3 or AAC (Advanced Audio Codec) file to a hard disk.

▸ **Burn Song to CD**—Burn a finished song directly to an audio CD. This feature is only available if your Mac can burn audio CDs.

Sharing Projects with iTunes

Exporting to iTunes is as simple as choosing Share > Song To iTunes. Before you begin exporting, however, you'll need to do a few things to prepare your songs. You'll set your GarageBand preferences to create a playlist in iTunes. Then you'll evaluate a song to make sure that you're exporting the whole song, and you'll check the output level for clipping. Finally, you'll export your song to a new playlist in iTunes.

Setting Preferences for iTunes

To prepare a song for export to iTunes, set your song and playlist information in the Export pane of GarageBand preferences. For these exercises, you'll use the Dog Walk Ditty song.

1   Open the project Lesson 9 > **9 Dog Walk Ditty**.

2   Choose GarageBand > Preferences to open the Preferences window.

3   Click the My Info button to open the My Info pane, if it's not already showing.

Next, you will name the iTunes playlist, composer, and album. By default, Garage-Band names the playlist and album after the registered user of the computer.

4   In the Composer and Artist Name fields, type your name. In the Album Name field, type *GB Book Album*. In the iTunes Playlist field, type *GarageBand*.

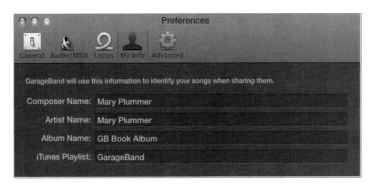

5   Click the Advanced button and make sure that the Auto Normalize checkbox is selected. Close the Preferences window.

The Auto Normalize feature is great for exporting songs to iTunes, because it auto-matically adjusts the volume level to make sure that the song will be loud enough to match the maximum volume levels of professional CDs.

Now that you've set up the export information, iTunes will automatically create a playlist titled GarageBand and include the other information in the playlist. Technically, this song was composed by me, but you contributed and this way the settings on your computer will be ready for the next song that you create in GarageBand.

Evaluating a Song's Output Level

You already fixed the output level of this song in the previous lesson, so it should be fine. However, when you are working with one of your own projects, always make sure that the loudest part of the song isn't clipping in the Master Output meter at the top of the Garage-Band window. If the meters peak in the red at any time, turn the level down until there is no red visible during playback.

Sending a Song to iTunes

When you export a song to iTunes, the entire song is exported, from the beginning of the first measure to the end of the last region. (If Cycle mode is on, only the portion of the time-line included in the cycle area is exported.) But, remember, if you mute or solo tracks, only those tracks set to play are exported. Let's export the current song to iTunes.

1   Choose Share > Song to iTunes to export the song.

The Share To iTunes dialog opens. Here you can choose to modify the playlist informa-tion. You can also select the Quality pop-up menu or select the "Export cycle area only, or length of selected regions" checkbox if you only want to export the cycle area or the length of selected regions.

The title has been modified to include the date and time after the project name. Let's delete the date and number 9 from the beginning of the title. Also, you can select the quality for your output depending on if you want to work with uncompressed (AIFF) files or compressed files of various quality levels. The default, Highest Quality (iTunes Plus, 256 kBit/s), is great for sharing or burning to CD. You can also use the lower quality choices if you want to fit more finished songs on a CD.

2   In the Title field, change the name to *Dog Walk Ditty*. Then click Share.

Your file *bounces* to iTunes (meaning it is mixed into a new audio file). iTunes opens automatically with your new song ready to play or already playing, depending on your iTunes settings.

TIP   You can use the lower resolution settings in the Quality pop-up menu when you need smaller audio files for simple projects such as a podcast or web distribution. The higher quality settings create larger files.

After your song has been sent to iTunes, you can access it from other Apple applications through the Media Browser. Let's try it.

3   Press Command-Q to quit iTunes. Select the GarageBand window to make it active, if necessary, and press F or choose View > Show Media Browser. The GarageBand playlist appears in the iTunes library of the Media Browser audio pane.

4   Click the GarageBand playlist to see the Dog Walk Ditty song in the list at the bottom of the Media Browser. Press the F key to hide the Media Browser.

NOTE ▶ Any tracks that are muted at the time you export will not be included in the song. This can work to your advantage if you want to make a practice version of a song that excludes certain instruments.

That's all there is to adding a song to iTunes and the Media Browser. Once in iTunes, you can burn your album, playlist, or individual song to a CD (if you have a burner), or convert it to another file format.

Sharing a Ringtone to iTunes

Sharing a ringtone is very similar to sharing a song. The difference is that it must be under 40 seconds in length, and there must be a cycle area designating the length of the ringtone. Finally, a ringtone is saved with a different file extension so that it will be recognized as a ringtone and can be synced to your phone.

1   Open the file **9 Loopy Ringtone** from the Lesson 9 folder. When prompted to save the changes to the previous project, click Save. The project opens with Cycle mode turned on.

2   Play the project. Listen to the full cycle area once and let it restart before stopping playback.

The song doesn't really loop as well it could for a ringtone. Let's shorten the cycle area to bar 17 so that the melody loop doesn't restart again (at bar 17).

3   Drag the right edge of the cycle area from bar 20 to bar 17.

4   Play the cycle area again to hear it loop. Perfect!

5   Choose Share > Ringtone to iTunes, and then quit iTunes. Save and close the project.

The ringtone will be added to the Tones in your iTunes library, and if you choose, you can sync it to your iPhone and use it as your ringtone.

Sending a Song to SoundCloud

If you already have a SoundCloud account, you can log in and share your songs to Sound-Cloud directly from GarageBand. If you don't have a SoundCloud account, you will be prompted to create one. Before sending a song to SoundCloud, you can choose the quality and visibility level for the shared song as well as set permissions. You also can send an email to notify others that the song is available.

MORE INFO ▶ You can find specific steps for sharing to SoundCloud in the GarageBand Help under Share projects > Share songs to SoundCloud.

Exporting a Project as a Movie

GarageBand projects that contain a movie file can be exported as movies with the project's audio as the audio track. Let's export the **9 RSD The Step Off** project as a QuickTime movie.

1   Open the project **9 RSD The Step Off** from the Lesson 9 folder. When prompted, locate the missing movie file in the Additional Media folder.

2   Choose File > Movie > Export Audio to Movie. A dialog opens for you to choose the location, name, and preset for the new movie that will be created.

3   Name the file *RSD The Step Off*. Choose Desktop for the location, and select Full Quality from the Preset pop-up menu.

The Full Quality setting will maintain the original video resolution and settings. The file size will be only 95.9 MB. Feel free to experiment with the other export settings after you finish this lesson.

The finished movie file appears on your computer desktop.

Fading Out the Master Track

One of the most important features of the master track is that it can be used to dynamically change the volume curve of the overall song. You can easily add control points to the master volume curve, just as you would to any other track. Instead, for this exercise, you'll use a handy fade-out feature.

For this exercise you'll add a fade to the Scales project you worked with in Lesson 1.

1   Open the project **9 Scales** from the Lesson 9 folder. Play the project once for nostalgia. Pay close attention to the ending.

The ending isn't very dramatic, or conclusive, so let's add a fade to the master track before sharing or exporting the project. You may also notice that I added a fade to the beginning of the Tambourine region so it eases into the music rather than popping in abruptly.

2   Choose Mix > Fade Out. Instantly the automation curves appear and you can see four control points at the end of the volume curve on the master track. You could move or delete some of these control points if you wanted to extend or shorten the length of the fade-out.

You can also see the control points I added to the Tambourine track.

3   Play the project to hear the fade-out to the master track. Then press A to hide the automation.

4   Save the project to your My GarageBand Projects folder.

As you can see, it is easy to fade out your project with a simple menu selection.

Exporting Songs to Disk

You may need to export a project to disk so that you can put it on a portable drive or email it to someone. In this exercise you'll export the Scales project to the desktop where you can then save it to a portable drive, email it, or use some other means of sharing the file.

1 Choose Share > Export Song to Disk. In the Export dialog change the name to *Scales*.

2 Choose Desktop as the location. Then choose the file format that you need, and specify the quality setting. Click Export, and the file will appear on your desktop.

TIP ▶ If you are creating a file for someone else, it's always a good idea to find out ahead of time what file format and quality or file size they need. If you aren't sure and neither are they, create multiple versions just in case.

Opening and Saving Projects via iCloud

For those of you who use iCloud to share files between your Mac and your iOS devices, GarageBand makes it easy. You can save a GarageBand project to iCloud using the Where pop-up menu right in the Save As dialog. Also, you can open a project from iCloud by choosing File > iCloud > Open iCloud Song.

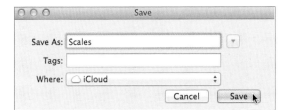

You'll learn more about iCloud and GarageBand for iOS in Bonus Lesson 2, "Working with GarageBand for iOS." Locate the bonus lesson on the same webpage as the lesson files.

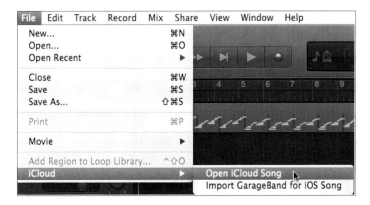

Project Tasks

It's your turn to share a project on your own. Open the project **9 Lifes Flower** and save it to your My GarageBand Projects folder. Play the project and adjust the music volume level (in the Event Horizon track) to your liking. Check the output level meter. If it seems low or high, raise or lower the Master Output level as needed. Change the My Info preferences so the artist is Tina Sacco. (It is really important to get credits right.)

Either share the project to iTunes or use the Export Song to Disk option. The muted tracks will not be mixed with the finished file. After you share the project, don't forget to go back to GarageBand Preferences and change the My Info preferences.

Congratulations! You have completed the sharing lesson and are ready to share, send, or export your own projects.

Lesson Review

1. What should you do to a music project before exporting it to iTunes?

2. What determines the length of the song file exported to iTunes?

3. Where do you set the information for exporting songs to iTunes?

4. What is the quickest way to gradually lower the volume (fade) at the end of a song?

5. How can you access iTunes files from GarageBand?

Answers

1. Check the master volume level to make sure the song is at a good level and not too low or too loud (no clipping).

2. The length of a song exported from GarageBand is its duration from the beginning of the first measure in the timeline to the end of the last region in the timeline. If you use a cycle region, only the portion of the timeline included in the region is exported.

3. You can set song and playlist information for iTunes in the GarageBand Preferences window.

4. You can choose Fade Out from the Mix menu to automatically add control points to the master track volume curve to slowly lower the volume at the end of a project.

5. In GarageBand and other Apple applications, you can access iTunes through the Media Browser.

Index

OS X Support Essentials 10.9

Supporting and Troubleshooting OS X Mavericks

Kevin M. White, Gordon Davisson

Lesson and media files available for download

Logic Pro X

Professional Audio Production

David Nahmani

Lesson and media files available for download

al Cut Pro X
d Edition

nal Video Editing

ynand

Lesson and media files included

The Apple Pro Training Series

Apple offers comprehensive certification programs for creative and IT professionals. The Apple Pro Training Series is both a self-paced learning tool and the official curriculum of the Apple Training and Certification program, used by Apple Authorized Training Centers around the world.

To see a complete range of Apple Pro Training Series books, videos and apps visit: **www.peachpit.com/appleprotraining**

Apple
Certified

Differentiate yourself. Get Apple certified.

Stand out from the crowd. Get recognized for your expertise by earning Apple Certified Pro status.

Why become an Apple Certified Pro?

Raise your earning potential. Studies show that certified professionals can earn more than their non-certified peers.

Distinguish yourself from others in your industry. Proven mastery of an application helps you stand out in a crowd.

Display your Apple Certification logo. With each certification you get a logo to display on business cards, resumés, and websites.

Publicize your certifications. Publish your certifications on the Apple Certified Professionals Registry (training. apple.com/certification/records) to connect with clients, schools, and employers.

Learning that matches your style.

Learn on your own with this Apple Pro Training Series book from Peachpit Press. Advanced titles and video training are also available for select topics.

Learn in a classroom at an Apple Authorized Training Center (AATC) from Apple Certified Trainers providing guidance.

Visit **training.apple.com** to find Apple training and certifications for:

OS X	Aperture
OS X Server	Pages
Final Cut Pro X	Numbers
Logic Pro X	Keynote

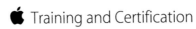 Training and Certification